INSTRUCTOR'S MANUAL to accompany

READING CRITICALLY, WRITING WELL

A Reader and Guide

FOURTH EDITION

Rise B. Axelrod

California State University,
San Bernardino

Charles R. Cooper

University of California,
San Diego

Kristin Hawkinson

University of California,
San Diego

ST. MARTIN'S PRESS
NEW YORK

For information, write:

St. Martin's Press, Inc.
175 Fifth Avenue
New York, NY 10010

ISBN: 0-312-11526-1

CONTENTS

Part 1 PURPOSE AND OVERVIEW OF THIS MANUAL

This *Instructor's Manual* supports teaching with *Reading Critically, Writing Well*, Fourth Edition. Beginning teachers will find comprehensive support for planning a course, presenting and discussing the readings, and giving and evaluating writing assignments. Experienced instructors will find varied resources to complement their teaching styles and to orient them quickly to the readings.

Part 2 of the manual offers a rationale for the basic features of the text, and Part 3 outlines alternative course plans. Part 4 presents basic teaching activities to support your work with this text, strategies like presenting and discussing readings, assigning journals, organizing students to work collaboratively, organizing workshops, conferencing, evaluating students' work, and managing the workload. Instead of giving general advice, we share specific strategies and activities we have developed in our own programs. If you are a beginning instructor, you will find Part 4 particularly helpful. It will enable you to approach your course confidently and to get good work from your students right away. Part 5 discusses ways to introduce the critical reading strategies presented in Chapter 1 of the text.

Part 6, the longest part, takes up each genre chapter (2–9) in turn, providing an orientation to the writing assignment at the core of the chapter, the sample essay that opens each chapter and the exercises based on it, an overview of readings, resources for teaching each reading, and comments on the guide to writing that closes each chapter.

To conclude the *Instructor's Manual*, Part 7 presents two bibliographies, one on composition studies, the other on learning from text.

Part 2 RATIONALE FOR THE BASIC FEATURES OF THE TEXT

This section explains briefly why we wrote *Reading Critically, Writing Well* the way we did. Our discussion of the ideas behind the text takes up the following topics:

- the relation between reading and writing in a writing course
- why critical reading strategies must be taught and how their practice contributes to writing development
- why students need a comprehensive framework of support as they draft and revise, with a focus on systematic invention
- the text's chapter sequence and relations among the chapters
- the possibilities for library and field research in a course using this text

RELATING READING AND WRITING BY GENRE

Schemas—memory for text—guide our reading and writing. Novice writers must develop schemas for the genres they will read and write in college and on the job. These schemas are learned through reading many essays in a genre, by analyzing selected essays rhetorically and stylistically, and by writing and revising essays with genre criteria in mind. Genre schema permit more confident, efficient reading and foster productive global planning during composing and revising.

We understand a genre to be a social construct that has evolved over time to meet writers' needs in recurring and now familiar writing situations. We consider genres to be heuristics that enable composing. While there can be a wide variation of form and strategy within a genre—as readings in each of this text's chapters illustrate—experienced readers and writers in a culture recognize paradigmatic instances. Genres are not fixed but change over time in response to a culture's changing rhetorical demands.

Current discourse theory and professional writers' experience confirm that each of the genres in Chapters 2–9—autobiography, observation, reflection, explanation of concepts, evaluation, speculation about causes or effects, proposal to solve a problem, and position paper—requires of students a special way of thinking and composing. In each genre, students must solve unique rhetorical problems and use information, memories, or arguments in particular ways.

We believe that, on their own, few students will discover the constraints and possibilities of our culture's key nonfiction genres. Unless they read widely and critically on their own or come from high schools with comprehensive writing programs where teachers understand the instructional implications of genre theory, students will need careful, focused instruction in the reading and writing of key genres. This text provides the materials, exercises, and assignments for such instruction.

This text relates reading and writing by genre. Students write autobiography as they are reading it, or they write proposals to solve problems as they are reading problem-solution essays. The readings collected in each of the readings chapters (2–9) illustrate a wide range of generic forms and strategies for development. Students observe many ways to begin, end, pattern, and develop a genre. They see writers solving predictable generic problems in different ways. This close matching of reading and writing by genre is the best way to realize fully the contribution reading can make to writing development in a composition course.

The text does more than simply match reading and writing by genre, however. An activity we call *Reading like a Writer,* which follows each reading, helps students understand the constraints and possibilities of a genre. They learn to read a genre—and they learn to read it as a writer does.

CRITICAL READING

The proven critical reading strategies we offer enable students to read more confidently and to get more out of their reading. Reading critically, we believe, is an approach—a stance—students can learn. Essentially, we teach students specific ways to act on a text and knowledge about how texts work.

We don't promise to make critical reading easy. In fact, we make reading harder and slower—but more productive. For every selection in the text, we invite students to read for meaning first and then to read like writers. And we ask them to read with pencil in hand, annotating the text from these two perspectives. Most important, we ask them to write about what they discover, using writing itself to explore ideas and to consolidate what they have

2

learned. Writing becomes part of critical reading—an essential activity of critical reading that provides a tentative record of meanings and insights stuents can then share with others and thereby further enlarge what they can learn from a text.

Briefly, we offer two stances of critical reading (reading for meaning and reading like a writer); three actions of reading critically (annotating, inventorying annotations, and extending writing); and several specific strategies of critical reading:

- previewing
- contextualizing
- questioning to understand and remember
- reflecting on challenges to your beliefs and values
- outlining and summarizing
- paraphrasing
- reflecting on challenges to your beliefs and values
- exploring the significance of figurative language
- looking for patterns of opposition
- evaluating the logic of an argument
- recognizing emotional manipulation
- judging the writer's credibility
- comparing and contrasting related readings

These critical reading strategies are collected in Appendix 1, A Catalog of Critical Reading Strategies. Annotating and inventorying are illustrated there, as well as in Chapter 1, which introduces students to our basic stances and actions.

The appendix strategies are gradually introduced to students following appropriate readings as they make their way through the book. They practice each strategy at least once and most strategies more than once. You may, of course, decide to have students use an appendix strategy with other appropriate readings.

This comprehensive, approachable, theory-based and research-supported program of critical reading provides no panacea, however. What students get from a reading depends in part on what they bring to it. (At the same time, students sometimes bring more to a reading than they imagine: that's where previewing and contextualizing come in.) We know that reading for meaning can be considerably enriched by discussion: textual meaning-making at its best is in part a social activity. While recognizing that reading depends on prior knowledge and is enhanced by sharing tentative meanings with others, we don't want to claim too much for what a text like this can do. At the same time, we have made it easy for you to help students preview and contextualize readings as you assign them and then to share their writing in response to the Reading for Meaning and Reading like a Writer activities following every reading.

There are three primary reasons for teaching strategies of critical reading in a college writing course: (1) a writing course in which readings play a major role should be a course in reading critically, (2) insightful critical reading is essential to writing development, and (3) research indicates that carefully taught and well-practiced critical reading strategies enable students to understand better and remember longer their reading and to use it more effectively in other situations, like writing.

WRITING INSTRUCTION

The pencil-in-hand critical reading strategies discussed in the preceding section contribute directly to students' writing development. Critical reading is necessary for writing development in that genre, but it is not sufficient. Students also need comprehensive support for invention, composing, and revising of a genre. This text provides such support through various activities and guides.

PRACTICING [THE NAME OF THE GENRE]: A COLLABORATIVE ACTIVITY. This activity, coming early in each chapter, enables students to practice the genre orally in a collaborative exercise that gives them confidence that they already know something about "writing it."

READING LIKE A WRITER ACTIVITIES. Students complete a full rhetorical analysis of each chapter's opening sample essay. In addition, they analyze a key rhetorical strategy of each reading in a chapter. If they complete these for every reading, they learn about all the basic writing strategies of a genre. What they learn greatly improves the chances for successful peer critique and workshop discussions. (Part 4 discusses methods of peer critique.)

CONSIDERING IDEAS FOR YOUR OWN WRITING. Following each reading in Chapters 2–9 is a section titled Considering Ideas for Your Own Writing, which offers many specific ways students can write in the genre they are learning to read critically. The ideas for writing present possible subjects within which students choose their own topics and find a focus for them. Attempting to write about the subject in a particular genre immediately engages students in analyzing the rhetorical situation. They must decide what their purpose is given their expected readers and determine what these readers are likely to know, think, and feel about a possible subject.

THINKING ABOUT WHAT MAKES [NAME OF GENRE] EFFECTIVE. In this activity, coming at the end of the readings and just before they begin working on the writing assignment, students review and consolidate everything they have learned about the rhetorical features of a genre.

GUIDES TO WRITING. Each assignment chapter (2–9) concludes with a concise but comprehensive guide to writing. This guide leads (and encourages) students through the process of invention, drafting, and revising. There now is solid evidence that guided, systematic invention enables school and college students to write better. Therefore, each chapter provides genre-specific invention activities that are based on established heuristics like freewriting, answering questions, list-making, outlining, and analyzing readers. Each activity requires only a few minutes (as few as one or two and rarely more than thirty). (See Part 4 of this manual for a discussion about assigning and encouraging invention.)

The invention activities, all of which involve some writing, enable students to find a topic, generate ideas about it, explore their writing situation fully, and even carry out any necessary research. These writings may record several days of a potentially rich invention process; students' first drafts are then longer, more thoughtful, more interesting, and closer to their best work on a topic. New to invention is a collaborative activity, Learning More About Your Readers, that helps students think more deeply about what their readers know and believe.

The guides also help students give and get critical readings of their drafts, set goals before and during drafting, and organize invention materials prior to drafting. Each guide concludes with advice about revising to strengthen the essay and improve its readability and with an invitation to reflect on what has been learned. The guides to critical reading and reflection are new to this edition.

These guides to writing complement the critical reading strategies. Together, they provide a comprehensive program in reading and writing. They bring reading and writing together in a way that gives every student a chance to become more literate.

CHAPTER SEQUENCE

Although the chapters in the text can be presented in different sequences (see the discussion of various course plans in Part 3), we offer here a brief rationale for the text sequence. These are the chapters:

Chapter 2: Autobiography
Chapter 3: Observation
Chapter 4: Reflection
Chapter 5: Explaining Concepts
Chapter 6: Evaluation
Chapter 7: Speculation about Causes or Effects
Chapter 8: Proposal to Solve a Problem
Chapter 9: Position Paper

In chapter clusters, the sequence moves from expressive, observational, and explanatory (2–5) to persuasive or argumentative (6–9) writing. While an autobiographical essay is not necessarily easier to write than a position paper, there are certain advantages to our sequence. Beginning with autobiography, firsthand observation, and reflection delays the need for finding and using secondary sources and for struggling with library research. Students work with familiar or immediate—though not necessarily very manageable—material. Strategies of description and narration practiced in autobiography are central to observation. The anecdotes important to autobiography and reflection can emerge again very usefully in certain arguments.

Both observation and explanation engage students in solving problems of presenting information that are central to all types of academic writing and to all forms of argument. These two genres may very well encompass the majority of writing situations in some academic and professional specialties.

Chapter 6 begins an argument sequence that comprises half the assignment chapters in the text. This sequence begins with evaluation and speculation about causes or effects because theorists of argument say that these genres are basic to all other forms of argument. For example, when students write a proposal to solve a problem in Chapter 8, they may argue the causes or effects of the problem and evaluate alternative solutions. Cause and evaluation can also be central to position papers on controversial issues.

The argument chapters emphasize strategies for devising plausible arguments for particular readers. The students' writing situation in each chapter can be viewed this way:

Chapter 6. demonstrating the validity of a judgment
Chapter 7. conjecturing about possible causes or effects
Chapter 8. arguing the feasibility of a solution to a problem
Chapter 9. defending a position on an issue

This sequence provides a challenging introduction to the critical reading and writing of arguments.

EMPHASIS ON LIBRARY AND FIELD RESEARCH

Since research can strengthen student writing in Chapters 3 and 5–9, the text regularly invites library or field research. In addition, Appendix 2 provides guidance with both kinds of research. Although research can be emphasized toward the end of a course, students have so much to learn about finding and evaluating sources, integrating sources into their essays, and citing sources properly that we believe they should be doing some research early in the course. Hence, the text features field research in Chapter 3, Observation, and library research in Chapter 5, Explaining Concepts. All subsequent chapters regularly invite students to do research. Such an emphasis on research provides a realistic introduction to writing in academic and professional specialties. Many of the readings, including student readings, use and cite sources.

Part 3   SUGGESTED COURSE PLANS

Composition instructors typically organize their courses around writing assignments. Since *Reading Critically, Writing Well* covers eight different genres and includes many ideas for writing in each genre chapter, it offers different possibilities for designing a course. This section describes a variety of course plans you can use as the basis of your own syllabus, beginning with a six-assignment plan. Then come plans for a two-semester program, a one-semester argument course, and a two-quarter program. Finally, we discuss the opportunities for research with the text, including the extended library-research paper.

ONE-SEMESTER PLAN: SIX ASSIGNMENTS

This plan permits six essay assignments from Chapters 2–9. Though this plan does not include a formal, extended research paper, many assignments invite or require limited research. For example, Chapter 4, Observation, requires field research (observing and interviewing), and Chapter 5, Explaining Concepts, invites students to research the concepts they write about.

From this plan, you could readily devise a syllabus for your course. A syllabus specifies for each class meeting the assignments, readings, and activities, with exact page references to the text.

All of the suggested course plans in this section assume that you might be requiring frequent writing in a journal, giving collaborative learning assignments, arranging in-class writing workshops for peer critiques of drafts, holding tutorial conferences over drafts, or assigning further reading. Part 4 offers advice on all such activities.

Here are the essay assignments, by chapter title, in this plan:

Autobiography
Observation
Reflection
Explaining Concepts
Evaluation
Proposal to Solve a Problem

This plan gives balanced attention to personal writing (Chapters 2, 4), explanatory writing (Chapters 3, 5), and argument (Chapters 6, 8). It uses all chapters except Chapter 7, Speculation about Causes or Effects, and Chapter 9, Position Paper. Chapters 7 or 9 could be substituted for Chapters 6 or 8.

Our impression is that most writing programs on the semester plan give five to seven major writing assignments. Along with work on the critical reading strategies and a revision of each essay, the six-assignment plan we propose here is quite full. This full plan can be reduced by dropping an assignment or expanded by adding one. Whatever the details of your own syllabus, our proposed plan suggests a manageable pace and a way to sequence and integrate activities.

Keeping in mind that each of our assignment chapters offers many critical readings and writing activities, you might want to allow as much as three weeks for each assignment, especially if you ask students to revise their essays. In that case, you would want to assign only five chapters, or perhaps even as few as four during a typical fourteen- or fifteen-week semester. Here's how one assignment sequence might play out over a three-week period in a class meeting three times weekly:

Week 1
M: Discuss chapter opening and writing situation
   Do group-inquiry activity
   Assign introductory reading, Exercise 1, and half of Exercise 2
W: Discuss Exercises 1 and 2
   Assign remainder of Exercise 2
F: Discuss Exercise 2
   Do first reading and reading activities in class
   Assign second and third readings and reading activities

Week 2
M: Discuss second and third readings
   Assign fourth and fifth readings and reading activities

W: Discuss fourth and fifth readings

Discuss possible essay topics in Ideas for Your Own Writing following each reading

Assign first half of invention in guide to writing

F: Evaluate essay topics

Review invention work

Assign remainder of invention work and first draft of essay

Week 3

M: Workshop on drafts

W: Workshop on drafts

Assign revision

F: Revision due

Introduce next assignment

TWO-SEMESTER PLAN: TEN ASSIGNMENTS

Several colleges use *Reading Critically, Writing Well* as the basic text, usually along with a handbook or one or more tradebooks, for a two-semester writing program. A capacious two-semester plan like the following allows multiple resources in certain chapters to be used to the fullest. Here we list a possible essay sequence, assuming a pattern of course activities and assignments like that of the one-semester plan detailed above.

Assignment	*Chapters*
1	2, Autobiography: Narrating an Event
2	2, Autobiography: Characterizing a Person
3	3, Observation
4	4, Reflection
5	5, Explaining Concepts
6	6, Evaluation
7	7, Speculation about Causes or Effects (speculating about causes)
8	7, Speculation about Causes or Effects (speculating about effects)
9	8, Proposal to Solve a Problem
10	9, Position Paper

SEMESTER PLAN FOR AN ARGUMENT COURSE

The text includes enough material on argument to fill out a one-semester course concerned solely with argument or persuasion:

Assignment	*Chapters*
1	6, Evaluation
2	7, Speculation about Causes or Effects (speculating about causes)
3	7, Speculation about Causes or Effects (speculating about effects)

4	8, Proposal to Solve a Problem
5	9, Position Paper (without research)
6	9, Position Paper (with research)

This plan could make good use of the critical reading strategy Evaluating an Argument in Appendix 1.

QUARTER PLAN: FOUR ASSIGNMENTS

One-quarter courses can accommodate four of our assignments, though we know of courses using our text that give three to five assignments. Many programs at quarter-system campuses require students to complete two quarters of composition.

A one-quarter program faces hard choices. A sampling of personal, explanatory, and persuasive writing might look like this:

Assignment	Chapters
1	2, Autobiography
2	3, Observation
3	8, Proposal to Solve a Problem
4	9, Position Paper

TWO-QUARTER PLAN: EIGHT ASSIGNMENTS

A two-quarter program, with four assignments each quarter, might be organized as follows:

Assignment	Chapters
1	2, Autobiography
2	3, Observation
3	4, Reflection
4	5, Explaining Concepts
5	6, Evaluation
6	7, Speculation about Causes or Effects
7	8, Proposal to Solve a Problem
8	9, Position Paper

WHAT ABOUT THE RESEARCH PAPER?

Except for the Chapter 3 observational essay, every essay arising from Chapters 2–9 can be completed without research. In fact, the ideas for writing following each reading and the finding a topic section at the beginning of the invention sequence of each writing guide are designed to suggest many possibilities for writing that allow students to rely on their own present knowledge, experience, and resources. At the same time, every chapter except

Autobiography and Reflection can engage students in research, if the instructor wishes. We expect at least limited research with nearly all of the assignments in our own programs. Here we briefly outline the possibilities.

Chapter 3, Observation: Visiting a place, observing, interviewing, taking notes

Chapter 5, Explaining Concepts: Library research on the concept students explain

Chapter 6, Evaluation: Reseeing, revising, or rereading the subject being evaluated and taking notes

Chapter 7, Speculation about Causes or Effects: Library research on the event, trend, or phenomena speculated about in order to describe it fully and to survey others' proposed causes or effects

Chapter 8, Proposal to Solve a Problem: Interviewing people to understand more fully a problem affecting them and to anticipate their preferred solutions; library research on methods of implementing a proposed solution

Chapter 9, Position Paper: Library research on an issue in order to define and describe it adequately and to assess others' positions

Appendix 2 of the text provides comprehensive support for both field (observing and interviewing) and library research.

If your program requires an extended library-research paper, the most likely candidates in the text are Chapters 5 or 9, the one explanatory, the other argumentative. These chapters, along with Library Research and Acknowledging Sources in Appendix 2, provide full support for an extended, documented essay. Any of our proposed plans above could be adjusted to allow time during the final three or four weeks of a course for a library-research paper.

Part 4   TEACHING ACTIVITIES FOR A COURSE USING THIS TEXT

This section outlines basic teaching activities to support your work with this text. These activities, we believe, are important to the success of any composition course, whatever the textbook or other materials.

If you are a beginning instructor, you will find this section particularly helpful. Along with a syllabus based on one of our course plans in Part 3, the activities outlined in this section permit you to organize a complete course from start to finish: schedule, assignments, classroom and homework activities, evaluation of student writing, and record-keeping.

Instead of offering general advice in this section, we share specific activities, assignments, and materials we presently use in our own programs. Between the two of us authors, we have accumulated (to our amazement) fifty-four years of teaching writing and administering writing programs at six colleges in California, Colorado, and New York. What follows presents the best we know about organizing and teaching a writing course.

Note: This section presents general teaching activities; the next sections (Part 5 and 6) provide specific support for teaching the introductory chapter and each genre chapter.

PRESENTING AND DISCUSSING READINGS

If students are to succeed with an essay assignment in one of our genre chapters, they should read—and critically reread—the readings in that chapter. They should compare and contrast readings in order to see the full range of possibilities for their own essay in a genre. Class discussions of readings should be focused, efficient, productive, and encouraging to students as writers. How might you ensure such critical reading and discussions? This section provides an answer.

GIVING CLEAR AND COMPLETE ASSIGNMENTS. Even in a casual, slow-moving course using *Reading Critically, Writing Well*, assignments will be frequent: both the writing and the reading must be moved along by almost daily student work. If you find our other recommendations in this section persuasive, there will be several complementary strands of work to be moved along simultaneously in your course, engaging students in a variety of out-of-class assignments each week.

We believe the most effective way to give assignments is to prepare carefully a once-a-week handout. Even though we give students a rather detailed course syllabus, we further detail assignments for each week. We put assignments in writing because students do not all hear the same thing, it seems, when we give assignments orally, and also because class time is not lost in dictating assignments or writing them on the board. The weekly handout precludes hasty last-minute assignments as students gather up books and head for the door. Most important, we think, preparing the weekly assignment handout gives us an opportunity to think through carefully what we want to accomplish in a given week.

Except for drafting and revising full essays, assignments in a course using this text are relatively brief. For example, a single reading and its reading activities might take an hour. Exploring in the journal an idea for writing following a reading might take ten or fifteen minutes. The introduction to each chapter might require two hours, time best divided into two or more working periods during one or two days. In the guide to writing in any genre chapter, invention work entails brief writings spread over two or three days. Such frequent writing—our goal for students is *daily* writing—lets the mind work on the readings, consolidate new rhetorical learning, and produce ideas for writing. Consequently, *frequency* and *variety* of writing are essential. Pacing of work during the week and from week to week is crucial. Your weekly assignment handout paces, sequences, and clarifies this work. Students' limited time is used efficiently, and they are prepared for class.

We give weekly assignments at the beginning of the first class meeting of each week and take a few minutes to go over the assignments and answer any questions. Because there is a handout, students who come late rarely take our time after class to discuss assignments. A student who must be absent can later pick up the assignment handout at the writing program office, or a friend in the class can take one for the absent student.

If you file your assignments in a personal computer, there is a substantial time savings the next time you teach the course. You can easily revise or move certain assignments.

Some of our instructors append brief comments to the assignment handout—reiterating course goals, previewing an especially challenging assignment, forecasting a change of pace, praising or exhorting, summarizing progress and anticipating next developments, relating concepts and assignments in order to give students a larger view of the course, and so on.

PREVIEWING READINGS. Most of the genre-chapter readings are preceded by previewing questions. These questions are designed to help students activate prior knowledge of the subject, discover the genre of the text, speculate about its historical or cultural context, or sample its content. These questions enrich readings, and they may also entice or invite students to read a reading. As you assign a reading, you can do still more, however, to entice students to read it:

> Tell them some things you may know about the historical or cultural context of the reading.
> Tell them something about the author, or read a brief excerpt from one of the author's books (for example, when you assign "A Chase" by Annie Dillard in Chapter 2, read a few of Dillard's arresting, memorable aphorisms and analogies about writing from her best-selling book *The Writing Life)*.
> Show them the book or an issue of the magazine from which the reading was selected and talk about the impact of the book or about what you learned from it, or explain the purpose and readership of the magazine.
> Preview what they will learn as a writer from the reading.
> Relate the reading to other readings in the chapter.

These enticements take only a few minutes, but they can increase students' willingness to begin a reading in the odd moments and places where homework gets done.

SETTING UP A READING JOURNAL. A reading journal and collaborative reading/learning assignments (described later in this section) are essential features of our courses. A reading journal differs from a personal journal, a writer's journal, or an exploratory "dialogic" (or "double-entry") journal in that it is concerned mainly or exclusively with using writing to learn about reading, with goal-focused journal tasks assigned by the instructor. For students keeping a reading journal in a course using this text, the frequent journal writings assist them in learning from their reading what a *writer* needs to know. This is a special kind of rhetorical learning. It is based on critical reading (and especially on critical rereading). Its mode is analytic and its outcome is conceptual. One of us has completed research (with Susan MacDonald) suggesting that in an assigned-readings course where a particular type of writing is to be the outcome, the reading journal we are proposing teaches students far more than an exploratory journal in which students initiate all the writing. (A dialogic or personal journal could be just the right choice in other learning situations.)

How do you set up a reading journal? After much trial and error over several years, here is what works best for us and our instructors. Students buy a special loose-leaf three-ring binder and label it *Reading Journal.* (We recommend an inexpensive version about a half-inch thick at the binder with a flexible cover—much more portable than heavy-duty binders.) Each journal assignment begins on a separate piece of paper labeled with the student's name, the date, and the source of the entry (Chapter 2, Dillard, Reading like a Writer), and any other information that will facilitate your record-keeping.

Give reading journal assignments once a week as part of your weekly assignment handout. Going week-by-week, rather than planning journal assignments for a longer period, gives you flexibility to speed or slow the pace; to insert assignments that arise from special problems or opportunities; and, most important, to match the assignments precisely to the week's sequence of reading and writing activities.

We collect loose-leaf journal entries every week or two and return them to students to insert in their binders at the next class meeting. The first time or two we spend more time reading and commenting than we will later: we want to be sure students know what we expect of their reading journals. If the entries are brief and thin, we insist on more writing in future journal entries. If the writing seems too serious, cautious, or planned, we encourage exploration, risk-taking, digressions, even playfulness.

If you number your journal assignments sequentially from beginning to end of your course and ask students to do the same in their journals, then you always know where each student is in the sequence and whether at the midpoint or end of the course students have completed all assignments.

Our instructors weight the reading journal 20 percent or 25 percent of the course grade. We tell students that they must complete all journal assignments in a timely fashion in order to receive a C in the course. We do not actually grade the journal. Instead, we skim it quickly at the end of the course and decide whether it is exemplary, very good, acceptable, or complete but thin and perfunctory, and inform students of our judgment in a brief final note. Some instructors record a plus, check, or minus in the response to each set of journal entries they examine during the course.

The goal is to spend as little time as possible reading journals and still encourage students to sustain their work in the journal.

How should students approach reading journal assignments? We outline various types of journal assignments below, each requiring a different approach. We can say in general, however, that journal writing is relatively informal. It is first-draft writing, not painstakingly planned, not tight or cautious. It is exploratory, discursive, digressive, associational. A student may begin a journal entry with one idea and end it with quite a different one. In the reading journal, a student *writes to learn,* not merely to report what has been learned.

Journal entries may (probably *should)* exhibit lined-out (less time-consuming than erasing) phrases or sentences, marginal or interlinear additions, one or more parts added later to the end. They should not strike the reader as perfunctory. Instead, there should be evidence of commitment to learning through writing, of insight, discovery, confusion, questioning.

What kinds of reading journal assignments might you give? We recommend three basic kinds:

1. Critical reading activities from Chapter 1 and the assignment chapters. Keep in mind that our critical reading activities—Reading for Meaning and Reading like a Writer—require writing. The reading journal collects and organizes *all* critical reading activities—no small convenience for you when, in a semester plan like the one we propose in Part 3 of this manual, students may complete thirty to forty critical reading activities during the course. The loose-leaf format enables students to exchange single entries and you to evaluate one or more activities at a time.

2. Copy and comment, as in the Commonplace Book, a staple of liberal arts education since the Middle Ages. Students occasionally copy a particularly striking sentence or brief passage from one of the readings and then comment/react/analyze for a page or so. You could assign copy/comment once with each genre chapter. In this way, our reading journal poses an activity prized by advocates of the dialogic journal.

3. Reflections on learning and on the course. Recent research demonstrates that when students step back and review what they are learning, they remember it longer and put it to better use. In a course using this text, students learn how to read and write certain genres; or, to put it another way, they acquire rhetorical or textual knowledge. As students complete each genre chapter and its essay, they could write a journal entry reflecting on what they have learned. Here is a journal task we use:

> Now that you have completed the work in Chapter 2, Autobiography, take twenty or thirty minutes to review all the materials you've produced for this assignment. Begin by reviewing Reading Autobiographical Essays: A Summary at the end of the chapter. Skim your invention work and essay draft, and then reread your revision. Finally, skim the writing you completed for the critical reading strategies following readings. Then write one and a half to two pages summing up what you've learned about reading and writing autobiography. Develop your explanation not in general terms *(interesting, coherent, organized, lively style)* but in terms specific to autobiography *(narration, pacing, tension or suspense, dialogue, specific narrative action, scene, point of view, concrete sensory details, dominant impression, autobiographical significance).* Use these terms in your discussion. Refer to particular readings and to your own writing (journal entries, invention, the essay). Your explanation can be more exploratory than decisive: write to figure out just what it is you learned. There's no need to plan carefully. Don't waste time worrying about what to write. Just identify one thing you've learned and start writing. Other things will occur to you as you write.

You can easily revise this example for a reflecting-on-learning journal task at the end of each genre chapter you assign. For later chapters in the text, you could add to this task the request that students bring along rhetorical knowledge from previous chapters. For example, students reflecting on what they have learned in Chapter 3, Observation, could be asked which rhetorical concepts from Chapter 2 informed their reading and writing of observational discourse, or students moving through the argument chapters (6–9) could be asked to compare and contrast the different types of argument.

Students might also be asked to comment on the course. With these tasks, you want to deflect personal evaluations of other students and of you and invite frank assessments of progress problems with assignments or materials, misunderstandings, special insights, frustrations. Questions like these, in various combinations, have worked very well for us:

> What has most surprised you so far about this course? Account for your surprise. (We ask this question and the next two early in a course.)
>
> What has most pleased you so far about this course? Most disappointed you? Account for your pleasure and disappointment.
>
> How is this course different from your high-school English courses, and how is it similar to them?
>
> How is this course influencing your reading and writing in your other courses? Give specific examples.

How are your reading and writing changing as a result of this course? Give specific
   examples.

We are now at the halfway point in the course. What are you most pleased with about
   your development as a reader and writer? What are your goals for the second half
   of the course?

What one thing could I do to make the course more satisfying for you? What one thing
   could you do? Explain why these changes could be important for you.

We like to pose a journal task like this every two weeks or so. From students' writing we learn a lot about the students and the course. You will readily think of other questions to ask as you get to know your students.

GIVING QUIZZES. For many years, we resisted quizzing students to discover whether they had completed our assignments, assuming they had developed a mature understanding of the consequences of neglecting reading assignments. Now we give a quiz at the beginning of most class meetings for which readings have been assigned. The reasons we changed our position are that (1) we came to recognize the competing demands on students' time, and (2) we gradually came to understand how important thoughtful critical reading is to students' development as writers. Therefore, we now provide every possible encouragement for students to complete reading assignments. Giving clear reading assignments, previewing readings enticingly, and giving reading journal assignments on the reading provide much of the encouragement. Quizzes provide the rest. Students rarely come to our reading-day discussions unprepared. And as a consequence, their essays are stronger because they are informed by rhetorical strategies from the assigned readings.

We rely on three basic quiz questions, which we give orally (we give only *one* for the quiz).

1. Tell me what you know about reading X.
2. Tell me what a writer can learn from reading Y. (For these two questions we choose one of the two or three assigned readings.)
3. Tell me how readings X and Y are alike and different. (For this question we choose two of the assigned readings.)

Students write quickly for no more than ten minutes. Students who are tardy or absent may not make up a missed quiz. We take up the quizzes and file them with other quizzes in a folder for each student. We do not grade or return them. Instead, we may periodically review these folders and write a note to (or chat with) a student whose quizzes are unsatisfactory. Most students write satisfactory quizzes. In one or two minutes, you can skim a quiz folder in order to tell any anxious student how well he or she is doing on the quizzes.

At the end of the course, you can just as quickly tell which students have consistently performed well on the quizzes. You can overlook one or two missing quizzes. We usually weight quizzes 10 percent of the final grade.

Early in the course you can read aloud a few outstanding quizzes to give students an idea of what you expect. Be firm about the quizzes. Tell students why you give them. And then treat them lightly within the context of the whole course: quizzes are only one small means toward a consequential end—better essays.

GIVING COLLABORATIVE LEARNING ASSIGNMENTS. There is a growing interest—and an expanding literature—in collaborative writing and learning. For twenty years or more in the schools there has been serious experimentation with collaborative learning. Most projects have been concerned with concept-learning in science or history. Studies and reviews of studies indicate that students learn more through carefully planned small-group activities.

Collaborative learning has always been central, of course, to writing workshop courses or to any composition course where students meet in or out of class to discuss work in progress. For quite a while now, experienced, informed writing instructors have seen themselves as collaborators with students to improve their composing.

And there is new interest within composition studies in collaborative *writing*—those occasions in academia, bureaucracies, and the professions when two or more writers collaborate to produce a single piece of writing. For the last two years a few of our instructors have occasionally given a collaborative writing assignment—usually in Chapter 7, Speculation about Causes or Effects, or Chapter 8, Proposal to Solve a Problem. One of them (M. A. Syverson) has researched the problems collaborative writing groups encounter and convinced us that we need to know much more about how to arrange collaborative writing assignments in order for freshmen to succeed with them.

We have few reservations, however, about the contribution collaborative *learning* can make to our program. We ask students to meet in small groups *outside of class* to discuss *readings* and elaborate and consolidate their learning of rhetorical and textual concepts. Each student reads assigned readings and then meets with his or her collaborative learning group to complete tasks we pose. These meetings are occasions primarily for rereading and talking, though some writing usually results as well. We sometimes talk about these groups as collaborative *reading* groups.

Here are our two basic activities. We try to assign one or the other in each genre chapter.

Group Report on a Reading

Carefully read the essay assigned to your group, complete the Reading for Meaning and Reading like a Writer activities, and then meet with your group to prepare a presentation for the rest of the class.

You will present what you have learned by sharing your Reading like a Writer responses, rereading the essay, and discussing what you've learned about the genre. What strategies did the writer use? What did you learn that will help when you are writing your essay?

In preparing your presentation with your group, you should review the summary at the end of the chapter. You may use these strategies as the focus of your discussion.

You should expect other members of the class to be familiar with the essay you will present. Needless to say, be sure that you are familiar with the essays assigned to the other groups. You must be prepared to participate in the discussion about the essays that the other groups present.

Group Evaluation of Two Readings

Your group has been assigned two readings. Carefully read the two assigned essays before you meet with your group. Before you read, though, review the summary at the end of each chapter where you find the readings. Then, as you read both readings, take notes on how they fulfill the basic features of the genre. Also complete the Reading Like a Writer activity at the end of each reading. Decide on your own which reading you think is the better example of the genre.

Then meet with your group and discuss each person's choice of the better example. Arrive at some consensus and prepare an oral report about your evaluation for the rest of the class.

In your report, you should explain your group's judgment and the reasons for making it. Be sure that you refer to the basic features of the genre. If one or two of you cannot agree with the other members of your group, feel free to file minority and majority reports.

You should expect other members of the class to be familiar with these essays. Likewise, be sure that you are familiar with the essays assigned to the other groups. You must be able to participate in the other groups' presentations of their evaluations.

You will see many possible variations on these basic activities. For example, for the evaluation of two-readings activity, you could ask groups to report on similarities and differences between the two readings rather than to argue that one is better.

How do you arrange collaborative reading groups? As soon as possible, assign each student to a group of four. You may have one group of three or five; but five have greater difficulty in finding a common meeting time than four, and three are sometimes reduced to two and then are not really a "group." If students drop out during the term, you may need to combine reduced groups. On what basis do you form these groups? Try to avoid homogeneous groupings. We recommend a mix of different genders, cultural backgrounds, age, or other factors that will ensure a heterogeneous group. You may also want to ensure a range of writing abilities in each group.

Give students a moment to meet in class to schedule a regular time to meet. They will need a two-hour time block when they can all meet outside of class.

Explain to them that the collaborative discussion of readings will contribute to their success in your course, and offer them general guidelines for collaboration. Their goal—at least in these two basic activities—is to prepare a brief report (five to eight minutes, depending on how many groups you have and how long your class meets) on what they learn about the readings. Tell them they must report as a *panel,* with each person contributing. Since the reports tend to sprawl, you will have to enforce time limits so that all groups may report and you will have time for other activities.

FACILITATING CLASSROOM DISCUSSION OF READINGS. The day arrives when students come to class to discuss the readings—a crucial moment in a course hoping to help students read critically and write well. This is potentially the *worst* moment in a writing course. Students look at the floor. No one volunteers to take your first question. The first person you call on wasn't able to do the reading. The second person you call on thought the readings were assigned for the next class meeting. The third person you call on seems to have misread or partially read the reading. The mood changes. You feel grim. The students feel embarrassed. What to do? Probably the only thing to do is to allow time for everyone to read a reading before you attempt to discuss it. As a result, only one of the three readings you assigned receives any attention.

This nightmare scenario will likely never be realized in your course if you include in your course planning and assignments the activities we have described in earlier sections:

Reading assignments given by you on a weekly handout

Motivation to read from your enticing previews

Reading journal assignments to complete the critical reading activities following assigned readings

A collaborative reading-group assignment on the readings

A quiz on the readings

Here's the plan we follow for a class meeting to learn as much as possible about assigned readings:

Quiz

Reading aloud of journal entries (two to four students), followed by discussion and/or

Collaborative learning group reports, followed by discussion and/or

Your own close reading of a text or a monologue from you on the context of a text, its author, its major ideas, and so on

Your own (or a student's) summary of readings/discussion in terms of rhetorical features of the type of writing and the students' writing task

Notice that even though students have prepared carefully and must contribute to the presentation and discussion of readings, there is still a major role for you to play. Experienced teachers can arrange for students to say most of what needs to be said about readings, but they can rarely get them to say *all* that needs to be said. And so you say what they are not yet prepared to say. You make connections that will not be apparent to them as they are beginning to study a genre. They especially need your help in looking closely at features of a particular essay. As they observe you reading critically—reading rhetorically, reading like a writer—they learn to do it themselves.

It is important to begin each discussion by reminding students of the purpose for discussing the readings: to examine the basic features of and writers' strategies in a particular genre and to improve students' own writing as a result of this examination. As the discussion progresses, keep reminding students of the connections between the various readings and their own writing.

As the discussion proceeds, keep summarizing the main points of your exploration of the reading, perhaps using the chalkboard. Remind students often of the relation between the reading and their own writing.

To complete the discussion of each reading, ask students to summarize the main things they have learned. This could be a quick, focused summary by one or two students. Some instructors go around the room, asking each student to make a brief summarizing comment on the essay. You can then reiterate the main points of the discussion, and help students to see the connections between each reading and the other readings.

End the discussion session by once again reiterating the basic features of the type of writing and the rhetorical strategies used in the essays you have discussed. An in-class journal question can help students focus and reflect on what they have learned during the discussion.

Give up on discussions that don't seem to be going anywhere or that aren't engaging most of the students. Do not stay on a single point (or a single essay) for too long. Instead, keep the pace of the discussion fairly quick so that students remain attentive.

Try to involve every student in every discussion so that a few students are not doing all the talking. Many students are somewhat shy about speaking in class, so this may take some special effort on your part. One way to elicit a spoken response from even the shyest of students is to ask a simple, low-key question such as, What do you remember best about this selection? Most students should be able to answer this question on the spot, and they can then be encouraged to speculate about why a certain feature makes the selection memorable.

ORGANIZING WORKSHOPS

The workshop brings class members together to read and respond to work in progress—usually first or second drafts of a piece of writing. In this section, we describe two workshop formats: (1) two students exchange drafts and write an analysis of each other's drafts, and (2) two or three students bring copies of their drafts for the whole class and then read their drafts aloud, followed by a whole-class discussion. In one of our programs, classes meet for two hours twice a week; consequently, we are able to use both formats on a workshop day, devoting about an hour to each one. Very likely your classes meet for an hour. In that case, you could use one or the other of our formats or use one at one class meeting and the other at the next.

WRITTEN ANALYSIS. In a two-hour workshop class, we typically begin by asking students to exchange drafts with another class member. Each student then spends the first forty-five or fifty minutes reading the partner's draft silently and writing a critical response to it. Questions to guide this process can be found under Reading [the genre of a chapter]: A Summary at the end of each genre chapter. As students first exchange drafts, they brief their partners on particular points they would like the partners to critique. They write their responses on separate sheets of paper, labeled at the top to look like this:

Autobiographical Essay Draft
Workshop Response for John Smith by Yolanda Jenkins

During the first part of the workshop, while students are working silently on each others' drafts, you may choose to move among them to offer advice. Alternatively, you can arrange in advance for students to bring copies of their drafts for you to review during this time. When students have finished their written responses, each partner returns the draft and response to the other, taking a minute to look over the response and ask the partner about anything confusing.

To facilitate this critical exchange, you may want to pair students according to their writing abilities, changing the pairs so that each student receives responses from several others during the course.

Student writers tend to write their first workshop responses with some anxiety. A few will launch into devastatingly honest evaluations of a partner's draft, but most err on the side of conciliation. Influenced perhaps by the knowledge that their own drafts are undergoing similar scrutiny, they are usually eager to praise and offer little substantial criticism. At the beginning of the course, they also lack the experience to make recommendations to the writer.

One way to address this problem in the first workshop is to take students through the summary questions at the end of each chapter, modeling for them the kind of critique that would let the writer know what works, what needs work, and what might be done about weaknesses. A good response points to specific things in the draft, describing their effect on the reader tactfully but honestly, and suggests options the writer might consider. Questions to the writer beginning with How about . . . ? are often useful. To model such a critique, you can use copies of a class member's draft or copies of an anonymous draft written for a similar assignment in a previous course.

Student pairs could arrange to meet outside of class, exchange drafts, and complete a written analysis. Arriving in class with analyses in hand, they could review and discuss them and then move on to analyzing still another student's draft in class or to discussion of a draft with the whole class. As attractive as this alternative may seem—it can save class time for other matters—it has not worked well for us. Student pairs do not seem to finish their drafts very far in advance of the workshop class itself, or one student in a pair finishes in time for the scheduled exchange of drafts and the other does not. All students seem to benefit from the same specific deadline: a draft must be completed by the time of the workshop class. In class, you can review with all of them the criteria for an analysis and coach them in making a useful analysis.

DISCUSSION. During the second hour of a workshop, we change the pace by moving to oral readings and responses. One format is to arrange in advance for one or two students to bring enough copies of their drafts for the other class members to share a copy between every two students. The writer tells the class about any particular problems he or she has had in the draft and then reads it aloud while the rest of the class follows along on the copies, making marginal notes where appropriate. The class will respond better if they hear and see the draft simultaneously. At the end of the oral reading, the instructor chairs a discussion of the draft, appointing a scribe to record specific suggestions for revisions on behalf of the writer. The questions in the end-of-chapter summary can form the basis of this discussion. At the end of the discussion, the scribe gives the writer the discussion notes and other students pass along their copies with marginal notes.

This whole-class discussion of one draft at a time simulates the traditional writers' workshop widely used in MFA programs. Many instructors using this workshop format ask that the writer not participate in the discussion. There are good reasons for this rule. At the draft stage, writers need to listen to the discussion, reflect thoughtfully on what readers say, why they misunderstand, what they have questions about. From listening to this sort of discussion of one's draft, a writer can know whether it struck readers as honest, engaging, authentic, informative, or convincing, especially if the readers also add further reactions in writing to copies of the draft as the discussion moves along and then return all of those copies to the writer at the end of the workshop.

You may choose to reverse our plan and begin a workshop class with whole-class discussion rather than with written analysis so that you can review the basic issues and requirements of the assignment. Even with the help of the guide to writing, there will still be students who have not quite brought the assignment into focus yet. By concentrating initially on one or two papers with the whole class, you can remind students of the basic issues of that kind of writing. At the end of the discussion, you can summarize these basic issues on the chalkboard and relate them to points in the end-of-chapter summary. This should give students more confidence in helping each other and keep them focused on the central rhetorical issues of the assignment rather than the peripheral ones.

Working with the whole class on one draft allows you to guide the discussion and make observations that are relevant to the assignment and not just to the draft in hand. An alternative is to divide the class into small groups of four or five, with one member of each group bringing copies of his or her draft for the others in the group and reading it aloud to them. In a large class, this allows more students to receive group responses to their drafts and encourages the more reticent students to participate in the discussion. You can join one group or move among the groups. This format works best when students know what is expected and can work productively without your guidance.

PRACTICAL CONSIDERATIONS. When a student comes to class late or without a draft, you have several options, depending on which workshop format the class is using:

Have the student work on his or her own draft
Have the student join a pair and read a draft page by page as one partner finishes
Have the student wait for another late student to show up
Have the student respond to a copy of a draft that has been duplicated for the whole class

In all these cases, the student must be reminded that he or she is responsible for obtaining another student's response to his or her own draft.

When the first and second draft of the same assignment are read in subsequent workshops, some instructors ask students to choose a different partner to respond to the second draft. Other instructors allow students to choose the same partner to read the second draft so that the partner can comment on the progress the writer has made since the first draft.

Some instructors find it useful to have students put their phone numbers on their workshop responses, so that writers can call their workshop partners if they find they have questions as they revise their drafts.

Some instructors ask all students to bring an extra copy of their drafts. During the pair-workshop, while pairs are quietly writing their critiques of each other's drafts, the instructor quickly reviews all drafts, looking for the obvious general problems.

HOLDING TUTORIAL CONFERENCES

Conferences with students are time-consuming and difficult to schedule when classes are large, but we recommend them highly as a teaching practice, even if you can see students individually only once or twice during the course. Conferences allow you to develop a rapport with students, thus building the trust and self-confidence that many students need before they will take the risks in their writing that lead to real progress. For many students, these conferences are their only opportunities to work individually with a college instructor.

A conference may be scheduled at any time during the composing process. We find it most useful after the first or second draft of an essay has been written, at a point when the student has spent some time thinking about the assignment, generating invention notes, and making at least one attempt to put the ideas into draft form but before the student has finished work on the essay. Ideally, the first draft is discussed in a conference and the second draft in a workshop with other students, or vice versa, before the student writes the final revision of the essay.

In the one-quarter courses we teach, we like to see students in conference three times. The second of these, the midterm conference, allows us to review the student's progress and discuss the goals for the remainder of the course.

INDIVIDUAL CONFERENCES. We find that the best length for individual conferences is half an hour, although it is possible to make some progress in twenty minutes if the time is spent carefully.

The student comes to the conference with a draft in hand and may at first expect you to play the role of mechanic, making the necessary repairs on it while he or she waits in anxious silence. It is often tempting to take the draft from the student and go to work on it, but this defeats the objective of conferencing, which is to help students learn to work on their own drafts. To this end, we leave the draft in the student's hands for most of the conference and usually begin by asking the student either to read it aloud or talk about it. In the most successful conferences, the students do at least half the talking; our comments merely draw them out and let them make discoveries for themselves.

Because our questions at the beginning of the conference, or after the student has read the draft aloud, tend to be the same, we give them to students in advance on a handout, leaving space between questions for their notes. This means that students come to the conference prepared with a list of things to say and questions to ask, and we can begin work immediately. Following are general questions we might ask students about their drafts:

1. What pleases you most about this draft? Which part seems most successful?
2. Which areas of the draft do you feel need work, and why? What would your toughest reader be likely to say about the draft?
3. Which were the hardest and easiest parts to write?
4. What did you notice when you read this draft aloud to a friend?
5. What have you learned from this assignment so far?
6. What changes are you considering for the next draft?
7. What new writing strategy were you trying to use in this draft?
8. What questions would you like to ask me about this draft?

Following are questions we ask students about a draft of an essay analyzing the causes of a trend. We tend to assign a trend, rather than an event or a phenomenon, options in Chapter 7. You could readily write such questions for any genre assignment.

1. What trend are you analyzing?
2. Why is it a trend, as opposed to a fad or a phenomenon?
3. What causes are you presenting to explain this trend? Which causes seem to you to be the strongest? Weakest?
4. Do you have a strongest or most convincing cause? Why have you selected this one particular cause as likely to be most convincing for your readers?
5. What have you done thus far in this assignment that you feel confident about? It can be anything from your research to the ideas you've developed to explain the trend you're writing about.

6. What problems are you having with this essay? Do they have to do with library research, listing possible causes, or evaluating causes? Are you unsure as to whether you are talking about a trend or a fad? In what specific ways can I help you?

Questions like these provide a good starting point for discussion, and they encourage students to take responsibility for their writing and assume an active role in improving it.

SMALL-GROUP CONFERENCES. An alternative to the individual conference is the small-group conference. Instead of meeting with each student for half an hour, the instructor meets with three students for an hour, spending twenty minutes on each student's draft. In a typical group conference, each student brings copies of the draft for the other two students and the instructor. They each read their drafts aloud while the listeners make notes on their copies. At the end of each reading, the instructor and the student talk about the draft. The other two students may quietly audit the discussion or contribute their views and suggestions. After twenty minutes, the writer collects the annotated copies and attention turns to the next student's draft.

The group conference lacks the privacy of an individual conference, an important consideration for shy students. On the other hand, the group may generate ideas that would not emerge in a one-on-one conference. Some of the comments we make about the first student's draft usually apply to the other two as well, and students often decide to change their own drafts after the discussion of another student's draft. Neither conference format is inherently better than the other; we recommend that you try both to decide which you prefer.

SCHEDULING CONFERENCES. One way of scheduling conferences is to have students sign up for time slots in the class meeting before conference week, writing down their names and phone numbers on a sheet that you can then post on the door of your office. If students find that they cannot keep the conference appointment, they go to the posted sheet and get the names and numbers of classmates who might change appointments with them. In this way, students are able to take care of rescheduling largely on their own, without having to call you.

One instructor finds it helpful to have students sign up for conference times *two* class meetings in advance—in pencil. She brings the list to the last meeting before the conference and circulates it once more so that students can double-check times and location and reschedule if necessary.

Students should be reminded to be on time for conference meetings, as even a few minutes can throw off your carefully planned schedule.

EVALUATING STUDENT WRITING, HANDLING THE PAPER LOAD, AND KEEPING RECORDS

Students completing an essay assignment will have generated a good deal of writing. We find it very important to have a system of accounting for all the writing turned in and a method of reading and responding to it that allows us to give students helpful feedback while processing the pile of student work in a reasonable amount of time.

At the beginning of the course, we give students a handout that specifies what they are to turn in for each writing assignment. Here is an example:

When you finish each assignment, you will turn in not only the final revision but *all* the writing you did for the assignment. Put this work in a file folder with your name, your section, and the assignment written clearly on the outside. Each folder you turn in should contain the following five parts:

1. *Invention:* Numerous pages of rough, unpolished invention from the Guide to Writing for the assignment in *Reading Critically, Writing Well.*
2. *Drafts:* Either one or two rough exploratory drafts, depending on the length of the assignment. They should be legible and labeled with your name, the assignment title, and the draft number. Number the pages.
3. *Workshop Response:* The response written on one of your drafts by a classmate during the workshop. The classmate's name should be on the response.
4. *Revision:* The final, revised version of the essay. This should be typed and proofread with any errors neatly corrected. Double-space, type on one side of the page only, and number each page. The title page should be labeled in the top right-hand corner like this:
     [Your name]
     [Chapter title for the assignment]
     Revision
     [Date]
5. *Reflecting on What You Have Learned:* Follow the guidelines in the activity of this name at the end of each assignment chapter.

This handout gives students a checklist of all the work they are to turn in. We find it reduces confusion, eases our management of the large amounts of writing, and speeds the reading and response process.

When we pull the handful of work from the student's folder, we skim to see that all the assigned writing is there and to see what the student has accomplished in the invention and drafts. The invention tends to be a good indicator of the depth and thoroughness of the revised essay, and problems in the revision can often be traced to deficiencies in the invention. We try to make this connection clear to students early in the course.

To keep track of the student's performance in the various stages of the composing process for each assignment, we keep a record sheet for the student. (An example of such a record sheet is at the end of this section.) This sheet is for our own records, and students do not see it. As we read the student's writing for each assignment, we make notes in the appropriate boxes on the record sheet. We find this helpful in reviewing each student's progress during the course.

The student's self-evaluation (Reflecting on What You Have Learned) asks them to reflect critically on their composing process, to think about what they have written, and to take responsibility for the decisions they have made. At its worst, a self-evaluation will say no more than "here it is—I like it—hope you do too," as the student declines the invitation to take responsibility. At its best, however, it provides the student with an account of his or her composing process, and it provides you with a critical introduction to the essay. It can also clearly indicate the student's level of involvement with the assignment. We usually read the self-evaluation carefully, after we skim the whole package.

We then spend several minutes on the revision. We make a few comments in the margins, noting both strong and weak points in the writing, and add a few sentences or a paragraph of comments at the end, on a separate sheet of paper. You may want to keep a copy of these comments for your own records. We try to find something in the essay to praise, and we find that critical comments work best when phrased in terms of what the student might have done in the essay or should try to do in the next one. Questions are useful, too, when they lead students to think about ways they might have addressed the problems in the paper. This approach casts the instructor in the role of expert adviser rather than hanging judge.

Our response to a student's essay is influenced by its location in the sequence of assignments. Our comments will be different in each of the following situations:

1. The student is to revise the essay one more time.
2. We plan to repeat the assignment.
3. The assignment will not be made again in the course, and we want to summarize the student's achievement.
4. The assignment is the first or last in a series of related writing assignments (for example, Chapters 6–9 on argument).

When time is limited, we respond to features in the essay in order of priority. In an autobiographical essay, we would begin by considering the larger rhetorical issues: what the writer has tried to accomplish in telling the story, its structure, the beginning and ending, and the pacing of the narrative. Next, we would look at some particular feature of the genre: the quantity and vividness of descriptive details, the writer's recollection of feelings at the time of the event or toward the person, the use of dialogue, and the proportion of narration, description, and commentary in the story. Finally, we would comment on the writer's style, diction, and sentence structure.

We do not comment on everything that could be improved in a paper. An inexperienced writer can be easily overwhelmed by too much criticism and become too discouraged to work on any of the problems. Rather, we try to focus on a few of the most important things that need attention, thereby giving the student achievable goals. We follow the same policy with mechanical errors and stylistic infelicities, assuming that if we mark every transgression in a weak writer's paper, the student will most likely attend to none of the problems. Instead, we mark every error in a particular section—a whole page or one or two paragraphs on a page—by placing a check mark in the margin next to the line where the error occurs. We put parentheses around long phrases or whole sentences that need to be revised. This conveys the message that the mechanics and style need serious attention, draws the student's attention to some particular examples, and saves us the bother of marking every mistake in the entire essay.

Then, most important, we ask students to identify and correct their mistakes. If you include the correction symbol from your handbook with each marginal check mark or set of parentheses, then students can go to the handbook for assistance in identifying the mistake and correcting it. We ask them to rewrite on the revision any sentence containing an error. If the error rate is high, a whole section may need to be rewritten. We check these rewrites as soon as possible, asking students to rewrite still again any errors that remain uncorrected. After two or three revisions have been marked and corrected in this way, we ask students to identify and analyze their own error patterns. They list and classify their errors, again using the handbook for assistance, and then write up briefly what they have learned. The result is that students begin to take responsibility for reducing error, syntactic garbles and awkwardness, and stylistic infelicities in their own writing—and they learn to use a handbook.

Finally, we do not hesitate to ask a student to revise still again an essay which fails to meet minimal requirements established by the readings and guide to writing in each chapter. This request sets standards more effectively than a low grade.

We do not grade individual essays. A letter grade is at best a cryptic indication of performance, and grades on individual essays can involve instructor and students in unproductive appeals and justifications. Furthermore, the risk of a low grade can discourage an inexperienced writer from taking creative chances. We recognize, however, that students need some indication of their progress before the obligatory letter grades at the end of the course, so we fill out for all students midterm progress reports with grades that indicate what they can expect at the end of the course if they continue at their present levels of performance. This form shows students where they need to focus their attention in the remainder of the course.

At the end of the course, we use a final course report form to write a response to the final essay submitted and an evaluative summary of the student's performance in the whole course. (Examples of these forms are included at the end of this section.) This summary, and the course grade, is based on a quick review of a student's revised essays—we ask that they be turned in along with the revision of the final essay. We also review our records of a student's attendance, reading journal entries, quizzes, workshop responses, and any other work we might have assigned. Then we give a final grade based on three criteria:

1. Whether all the assigned work has been completed in a timely fashion.
2. Whether the work has improved during the course.
3. Whether revised essays are fully realized rhetorically; that is, whether the student's revisions reveal substantial learning about the rhetorical and composing possibilities of the various genres assigned in the course.

Keep in mind that standards of success on the assignments in *Reading Critically, Writing Well* are comprehensively established by the readings in each chapter, the activities at the beginning of each chapter and following each reading, the guide to writing at the end of each chapter, and Reading a Draft Critically.

While we look at all of a student's revisions again at the end of the course, we might go still further and put in place a formal "portfolio" requirement. There is considerable interest now in portfolio assessment—in both high schools and colleges. Portfolios might serve two evaluation goals in a college writing program: (1) giving individual grades, and (2) establishing program-wide standards.

Here is a possible portfolio scheme that could work well in a writing course like the one we have described in this manual:

1. Students arrange a portfolio of their work to give you at the end of the course.

A number of types of collections are possible:
All revisions
All revisions and one of them revised still further

A small selection of the best work, to include at least one revision, one workshop response, one complete writing process (invention, drafts, revision), and some small number of reading journal entries. (You will no doubt think of other variations.)

2. Students write you a thoughtful letter commenting on their portfolio work. You would want to provide careful guidelines for the letter. The purpose of the letter would be to engage students in thoughtful reflection on the whole course.

3. You review the portfolio and respond in writing.

The portfolio, especially if it includes further revised work, might be the culminating assignment in your course, replacing an essay assignment. Students could confer with each other and with you about portfolio selections and about further revision of one essay.

You could exchange and discuss portfolios with other instructors in your program. With coordination from your program director, these exchanges could serve the purpose of greater uniformity in final course grades.

Course _____ Student _____

Section _____ Midterm Grade _____ Final Grade _____

Assignment	Topic	Invention	Drafts	Workshop Response	Self-Evaluation	Revision
Autobiography						
Observation						
Reflection						
Explanation						
Evaluation						
Proposal						

MIDTERM PROGRESS REPORT

Student_____   Instructor_____

Course_____   Date_____

Semester_____   Section_____

Quantity of Work. Has the student completed all the assignments?

Invention_____

Drafts & Revisions_____

Quizzes _____

Workshop Responses_____

Critical Reading Activities_____

Self-Evaluations_____

Attendance_____

Quality of Work. Has the student:

Used the guides to writing creatively?_____

Revised drafts substantially?_____

Given helpful workshop responses?_____

Written perceptive self-evaluations?_____

Edited and proofread carefully?_____

Completed thoughtfully the critical reading activities?_____

Participated in class discussions?_____

These areas need special attention in the remainder of the course:

Midterm Grade _____

FINAL COURSE REPORT

Student_____   Instructor_____

Course_____   Date_____

Semester_____   Section_____

Remarks on Final Essay

_____

_____

_____

_____

_____

_____

_____

Remarks on Whole Course

_____

_____

_____

_____

_____

_____

_____

Final Grade_____

We believe our introductory chapter to be approachable and not a sentence longer than it needs to be to introduce students to what we mean by "reading critically" and "writing well." Because this chapter introduces so many concepts and activities that will be essential to students' success in the course, we recommend spending a substantial amount of time in and outside of class working with the material presented in the chapter. Many of our instructors spend at least the first week of a ten-week term on Chapter 1, and refer students back to it whenever appropriate throughout the course.

The chapter offers six activities:
    1. Reflecting on Your Own Past Reading Experience
    2. Practice in Reading Critically
        2a. Reading for Meaning
        2b. Reading like a Writer
    3. Reflecting on Your Own Writing Experience
    4. Previewing the Writing Assignments
    5. Previewing a Guide to Writing

Activities 1 and 3 through 6 ask students to either preview the text or write about their own reading and writing experiences. Activities 2a and 2b introduce students to the two critical reading activities that follow every reading in *Reading Critically, Writing Well*: Reading for Meaning and Reading like a Writer.

DEMONSTRATING READING CRITICALLY

Using an essay, "The Dirty Secret in Fraternity Drinking Songs," that takes a position on a controversial issue, we demonstrate annotating, first as it might appear when reading for meaning and then as it might appear when reading like a writer. For each of these ways of reading, we show how exploratory writing can develop ideas. It looks simple enough in our demonstration, but it's actually harder to do well than it first appears. Consequently, you will want to help students attend carefully as you talk them through the demonstration. Following our demonstration of annotation and exploratory writing for both reading for meaning and reading like a writer, we provide students with a second sample essay, "There Is No Safe Sex." Here, in Activities 2a and 2b, students will have a chance to practice on their own the strategies we've demonstrated for them.

READING FOR MEANING: DEMONSTRATION OF ANNOTATION. Here, we introduce students to annotating, a strategy central to the making of meaning from texts. While many students are accustomed to highlighting as they read, we find this method is rarely adequate. Instead, students need to be guided to read more closely and mark their texts more discriminately. The annotated sample essay following the introductory discussion of annotation demonstrates one student's annotations for meaning; students should note that the student is responding here to the *content* of the selection, defining unfamiliar terms, keeping a running summary, and responding on a personal basis to the essay.

READING FOR MEANING: DEMONSTRATION OF EXPLORATORY WRITING. In this section, we show students how, using annotation as a starting point, a reader continues to clarify and extend his or her understanding of a text by writing about it. It's important for students to notice two things about our sample of exploratory writing: First, like the annotations on which it is based, it is a response to the content of the essay; second, in the same way that there are no "right" or "wrong" ways to annotate, there is no preexisting standard for exploratory writing. While the reader's exploratory paragraphs show the development of her understanding since she made the earlier annotations on the text, she has not attempted to come to any distinct conclusion about the essay. At this stage, the reader is still responding on a personal basis, asking questions, speculating about the authors' purpose, and registering surprise (and occasionally confusion).

READING LIKE A WRITER: DEMONSTRATION OF ANNOTATION. Students may need a considerable amount of guidance in making the crucial transition from reading for meaning to reading like writers. By walking them very carefully through this demonstration, you can help them understand the difference between these two ways of reading. The same sample essay appears following the introduction to this section, this time with the addition of annotations from a writer's point of view. Be sure students notice that, rather than responding to the content of the essay, the reader's annotations address the rhetorical strategies used by the authors and the basic features of this type of writing.

READING LIKE A WRITER: DEMONSTRATION OF EXPLORATORY WRITING. Students may already have noted that the student reader's second set of annotations not only identify the basic features of writing to take a position but also begin to comment on how well the writers' strategies achieve the goals of this type of writing. The exploratory writing demonstrates the student reader's developing analysis of each of the basic features of the essay, as well as her evaluative comments on how well the essay achieves its purpose. You can point out to students that even a very brief examination of each basic feature of the essay helps the reader to extend her understanding of the essay.

PRACTICING READING CRITICALLY

Once you have guided students carefully through the demonstrations of annotating and exploratory writing for both reading for meaning and reading like a writer, students should be ready to practice these strategies on their own. For this purpose, we provide a second position essay, "There Is No Safe Sex," by Robert C. Noble. Following the pattern of activities established in the previous demonstration, students will annotate and do exploratory writing based on their reading for meaning; then they will annotate and complete the exploratory writing task based on their reading like writers. Let students know that these exercises are prototypes of the exercises that will follow each reading selection throughout the text. You will want to have students at least start these exercises in class so that you can be readily available to provide guidance and encouragement. With patient coaching from you, students will persist with these exercises, and they will be prepared for extraordinary engagement with the readings in Chapters 2–9.

READING FOR MEANING. Here, we ask students to annotate Noble's essay for meaning and to explore in writing their understanding of the essay based on their annotations. We expect students to be able to write at least a page in response to the essay; you might remind students that the more thorough their annotations, the more readily they'll be able to generate substantial exploratory writing. Even with the specific suggestions we offer to help students sustain their exploration, you may find that some students need to be steered away from mere summary. We find that students do tend to have fairly strong personal responses to Noble's argument; they may need to be reassured that these types of responses are appropriate at this stage of the reading process.

New to this edition is an optional Reading for Meaning activity, Extending Meaning through Conversation. Should you decide to use it later, you will want to have students practice it now. Follow up by discussing with students what meanings seemed to emerge during conversation, what consensus was reached, what differences remain, and how in general conversation complements making meaning on your own.

READING LIKE A WRITER. Making the transition from reading for meaning to reading like writers may prove to be a hurdle even for your best students. Because this transition is so critical, be prepared to provide extra guidance in the form of class discussions and individual coaching at this stage to help students get the most out of the specific guidance provided by the text.

Once again, we ask students to annotate Noble's essay, this time focusing not on the content but on the basic features of the essay and the strategies the writer uses to achieve his purpose. We name the three most basic features of this type of writing and provide specific guidelines for analyzing each feature as it appears in the essay. While this exercise by no means provides the basis for a truly comprehensive analysis of a position paper, it offers students an accessible introduction to the kinds of thinking involved in reading like a writer.

Defining the Issue. This task asks students to look for two things: the writer's definition of the issue, and the writer's indication of the issue's significance. Because Noble tends to present the issue in black-and-white, all-or-nothing terms, students should have little difficulty responding to this task.

Asserting a Position. Noble makes his position abundantly clear, avoiding qualifying or limiting it in any way. Some students will appreciate his rather surprising identification with the "prude" in his first paragraph. Noble's references to the "perky, fresh-faced teenage girl," the "young, attractive woman," and the "sweet and gentle" gay AIDS victims who represent the "opposing position" may strike some students as being somewhat condescending.

Arguing Directly for the Position. Once again, this is a two-part task, asking students both to identify and to evaluate the evidence Noble presents. Students should readily note that Noble draws on a range of types of evidence, including statistics, anecdotes, and quotations from authorities. Even students who disagree with Noble's position will be likely to accept the authority of his evidence.

We recommend that you collect students' written responses to these exercises, reading them quickly and making occasional comments. Although you will want to record some form of credit for students as they complete the exercises, there is no need to evaluate closely or grade their responses. Collecting student responses to these exercises in Chapter 1 and checking them quickly sets a precedent near the beginning of the course, letting students know that you take their work seriously.

PREVIEWING WRITING WELL

Most of the material in this section serves as a preview for students of the guides to writing in each of the upcoming assignment chapters. Besides inviting students to scrutinize their own experience as writers, this section encourages students to begin to familiarize themselves with the textbook.

Part 6 TEACHING THE ASSIGNMENT CHAPTERS (2–9)

This section provides suggestions for teaching Chapters 2–9, the text chapters with readings and the major writing assignments. Each of these chapters opens with a guide to reading and closes with a guide to writing.

USING THE CHAPTER INTRODUCTIONS AND GUIDES TO READING

Each assignment-chapter introduction includes the following features:

- description of the type of writing, including comparisons or contrasts with related types
- the writing assignment
- academic and professional writing situations
- a collaborative activity that actively engages students with the rhetorical situation of the essay they will write
- a guide to reading the type of writing, which offers a reading selection and two critical reading activities: Reading for Meaning and Reading like a Writer

These activities provide students with a full introduction to the genre they will be reading and writing. Most important, the reading selection and critical reading activities together illustrate for students the work they will do with each reading selection in the chapter. There is one small but significant difference, however: here the Reading like a Writer activity surveys all of the major features of the genre, while the same activity following each chapter reading singles out only one salient genre feature of that reading.

ILLUSTRATIVE ACADEMIC AND PROFESSIONAL WRITING SITUATIONS. Each chapter opens with typical writing assignments from college courses across the disciplines and from professional life. We made up very few of the academic assignments: nearly all came from current academic texts or instructor's manuals. We did revise several of them to foreground aspects of the rhetorical situation, making explicit what the student is expected to know and do. Unfortunately, not all academics consistently make clear to students what is required in essay-exam questions or paper topics.

There is much you can do to involve students in analyzing these academic assignments. Here are two examples:

You can analyze one for them, emphasizing all of its thinking/writing demands and then they can analyze another (either in small groups or as a class)

You can ask each student to find another assignment in a textbook in another course or to construct a likely one based on information in the textbook

COLLABORATIVE ACTIVITY. Practicing [name of the genre]: A Collaborative Activity engages students immediately in an interactive, oral rehearsal of the situation they will encounter when they write the chapter's essay assignment.

You'll notice that each collaborative activity divides distinctly into two parts: first, the rehearsal of the writing situation, and second, a reflection on what happened and what students learned. You may have to help students make this shift. The whole activity need not take more than twenty minutes or so. Because students *experience* the writing situation early in the chapter, we have found they are much more interested in the readings and questions. It starts them into a chapter in a surprisingly productive way. Don't skip this activity!

THE CRITICAL READING ACTIVITIES. As we recommend in Part 3 of this manual, you can easily devote two one-hour class meetings to these exercises. Don't rush these. First-year students have very little experience with close textual analysis, and what they have to learn about each of our genres will be a revelation to them.

While the activities presented in Reading for Meaning are quite flexible, those suggested in Reading like a Writer go after specific textual information. You might do one or two parts together in class when you assign Reading like a Writer, just to get everyone started. Or you could give students time in groups of two or three to help each other make notes toward an answer they will later write up individually.

Students will need encouragement. They may not go deep enough at first in their rhetorical analysis, but if you select and read aloud two or three strong answers to certain parts of Reading like a Writer, they will get the idea.

ASSISTING STUDENTS IN USING EACH CHAPTER'S GUIDE TO WRITING

Every assignment chapter concludes with a guide to writing that leads students through a systematic composing process. Each guide is divided into four parts: Invention, Drafting, Reading a Draft Critically, and Revising. Here are some suggestions for integrating instruction on the writing process into a course on critical reading.

ENCOURAGING INVENTION. Many of your students may never have met the term *invention* before, and they may not immediately see the benefits of prewriting. To the inexperienced writer, writing prior to drafting can look like needless busywork. Consequently, students may be tempted to skip this stage of the composing process; if you stress the need to complete it, they may even be tempted to do the invention procedures *after* they have drafted their essays. While doing invention activities after drafting and before revising can be of use, it obviously defeats the objective of invention.

Each guide includes a sequence of invention activities designed specifically to help students ask themselves questions and generate ideas and information useful for their essays. Since so few students have ever participated in systematic invention, we are especially careful to introduce them to the invention activities. We ask the students to open their books to the invention section and then briefly explain the purpose of each activity. By having students turn the pages and skim the invention exercises while you preview them orally for the students, you will be able to reduce their apprehension about these unfamiliar activities and greatly increase the probability that they will successfully complete the invention section before beginning their draft.

This is also the time to remind students of the time-frame for invention: suggest that they begin work right away, but spread the work out over several sessions; tell them what day the invention will be due, and that you will be checking it on that day to ensure that their invention base is adequate to begin planning and drafting.

You could do the first part of the invention, Finding a Subject, in class as whole-class brainstorming or in small groups, beginning with suggestions in the book (including those in Ideas for Your Own Writing following each reading) and then move to choosing a subject and exploring it. Students will progress through the invention sequence at different rates, but you can help them stay on track by requiring that they reach a certain point by a certain class meeting. If you ask them to bring their invention-in-progress to every class meeting, you can ask them to share certain sections with their peers in pairs or small groups, while you circulate and examine each student's work-to-date.

Research is comfortably included in our broad definition of invention—everything that happens before and during writing to produce ideas and evaluate them. Except for the writing assignments in Chapters 2 and 4, all the other writing assignments can include formal research. Where research is appropriate, the guide to writing invites it. You can decide how much research students should do or leave it to them to decide. We provide additional guidance in Appendix 2.

MAKING DRAFTING PRODUCTIVE. Invention may produce a number of complete paragraphs, several lists, freewriting, an interview, or notes on library research—a plethora of material that must be organized before the student can write a draft. This much material poses for many students a new problem: what to do with all of it.

The guide to writing in each chapter urges students to consider several alternative plans before settling on one. Often students are unaware of alternatives; we find it helpful to illustrate several, sometimes from the reading selections and sometimes from topics suggested by students.

Each planning section reminds students, as they go on to draft, that what they have developed is only a plan. In other words, it is expendable. The final test for the paper is not whether it follows the outline, but whether it works. Like many other parts of the guide to writing, this may demand from inexperienced writers a new approach, a new order of priorities.

Up to the drafting stage, the student has been dealing with pieces or facets; now for the first time the student will attempt to see the material as a whole. We suggest that students write their first rough drafts in a single sitting lasting about two to three hours. The drafting session resembles extended freewriting: it lasts longer, it allows the student to pause much more, and of course the writer is trying for a more ordered product; but as in freewriting, the writer should work as fast as possible and not worry too much about grammatical details or spelling.

The objective of this approach is to keep the student focused on the larger shape of the essay, not on distracting details. Research shows that most competent writers occasionally write garbled sentences in their first drafts and that writers who struggle to perfect each sentence as it is written are inefficient. Of course, there are exceptions, and students should remember that the guide to writing is just that—a guide, not a set of inflexible orders.

GIVING AND GETTING CRITICAL COMMENTS. New to this edition is a comprehensive guide to advising another writer about how to improve a draft. It is titled Reading a Draft Critically, and it poses a truly valuable critical reading task for students, especially those who have experience only with simplified all-purpose peer-critique guidelines, often in checklist form.

The goal is to get students to read a draft closely in light of what they have learned about the genre and to write a couple of pages that describe the text, evaluating it using criteria appropriate to the genre, and advise on possible revisions. Framing the student's work in this chapter, the analysis is organized around the genre features introduced at the very beginning. See Organizing Workshops in Part 4 of this manual for ways to use Reading a Draft Critically.

We would stress here that without coaching and modeling, students will not be able to realize the benefits of giving and getting a critical reading with our guidelines. Therefore we recommend that you talk them through at least one step of the analysis the first time you assign a critical reading. When they complete their first critical reading of each others' drafts, you can then select some expansive, helpful sections of analysis to share with them as examples of what you expect from all of them.

PLANNING TO REVISE. Research has shown that successful revising depends on what the writer knows about the type of discourse. The more examples novice writers have seen, the larger the repertoire of strategies they can draw upon to achieve their particular purpose for their readers. When revising, writers must also keep their focus on global issues rather than sentence-level errors and infelicities. In teaching students to revise, peer critique and student-teacher conferences are invaluable.

For information on class activities to support students' revising, see Organizing Workshops and Holding Tutorial Conferences in Part 4 of this manual.

REFLECTING ON THE LEARNING PROCESS. Each guide to writing concludes with an activity that asks students to reflect on what they have learned about reading and writing in a particular genre. It is titled Reflecting on What You Have Learned. You may need to encourage students to write full, demanding, detailed reflections on their reading and writing experiences. After you assign this activity as homework, you might give them five minutes of class time, the day the assignment is due, to develop and expand on their reflections. Some additional coaching can also be very useful. Sometimes you need to help students see that every aspect of the process, from reading through invention, drafting, and revising, can be revealing. If students reflect in thoughtful detail on their own reading and writing processes, they can learn much about how they read and write. Students' responses to this activity can also help guide your own comments on their papers. The student who has written a miserable paper, and is miserable about it, might get very different treatment from one who has done poorly but is uncritical. We believe that there is pedagogical value in responding directly to the student's reflections so that the teacher's comments are not self-contained, but are part of a dialogue about the paper.

Chapter 2 AUTOBIOGRAPHY

Students should find the readings in this chapter accessible and engaging, but the point emphasized in the introduction to the chapter is that autobiography is more than just entertaining storytelling: it is an attempt to find meaning in experience. The selections in this chapter and the questions that follow them aim to show students that autobiography requires writers not merely to present people, places, and events, but also to interpret these subjects—to reveal their causes and implications and draw conclusions about them.

In learning about autobiographical writing, students are engaged in a fundamental process of discourse—making meaning from experience. In autobiography, the experience and its significance may be personal to the writer, but readers can recognize, believe, and understand this significance by virtue of common human ties. In drawing conclusions from their experience and supporting these conclusions with illustrative examples, students will be engaged in the kinds of composing they will encounter repeatedly in *Reading Critically, Writing Well*. In Chapter 3, for instance, students will see writers sharing their observations of life around them and drawing or implying conclusions about these observations. Chapters 2 and 3, therefore, represent a movement from writing that focuses on the self and relies on memory to writing that focuses on the world and relies on fresh observations and on-the-spot notes.

WRITING ASSIGNMENT: Autobiography
Here is the writing assignment that appears near the beginning of Chapter 2:

Write an autobiographical essay about a significant event, phase, or person in your life. Choose a topic with your readers in mind, one that you feel comfortable disclosing to others and that could lead them to reflect on their own lives.

Present your experience dramatically and vividly so readers can imagine what it was like for you. Through your choice of words and details, convey the meaning and importance—what we call the *autobiographical significance*—of this event, phase, or person in your life.

Possible topic ideas (Considering Ideas for Your Own Writing) follow each reading. A general list of topics is also included as part of the Invention section in the Guide to Autobiographical Writing.

Autobiographical Writing Situations

The three brief descriptions of writing situations for remembered events, phases, and people show students a range of possible occasions for this sort of writing. The three examples illustrate the role of autobiographical writing in both academic and nonacademic settings and also suggest a range of different purposes for autobiographical writing. You might want to use the situations in a discussion of possible topics by pointing out how the writers have chosen personally significant topics, how they have enough emotional distance from these topics to be able to discuss their significance, and how they achieve the self-disclosure and depth of insight for which students writing this assignment should aim.

Practicing Autobiography: A Collaborative Activity

If you are beginning the course with this chapter, this group activity provides a particularly good starting point. It has students tell each other stories—something everyone enjoys—and it gives students a chance to get to know one another and to begin forming good working relationships. But wherever this chapter falls in your course, this activity is a very effective way of introducing the assignment. It will increase students' interest in the chapter and their confidence that they will be able to write effective essays about remembered events, phases, or people. This activity guides students through a rehearsal for the essays they will later write and prepares them to think seriously about autobiography. Because students *experience* the writing situation early in the chapter, we have found that they are much more interested in the readings and activities. It starts them into a chapter in a surprisingly productive way, and is well worth the time it takes.

This activity divides distinctly into two parts: first, the rehearsal of the writing situation and, second, a reflection on what happened and what students learned. You may have to help students make that shift. The whole activity need not take more than twenty minutes or so.

In this chapter, the activity gives students direct, hands-on practice with the issues of purpose and audience they will encounter throughout their reading and writing for this assignment. Specifically, it will ask them to experiment with making topic choices, with telling a vivid story and presenting scenes and people, and with disclosing the autobiographical significance of their topics. As they reflect (as a group, but perhaps also individually) on their experience of telling their own stories and listening to those of others, students will begin to anticipate both the challenges and the rewards facing them as both readers and writers of autobiography.

A GUIDE TO READING AUTOBIOGRAPHY

This section introduces students to the critical reading and writing strategies they will use throughout the chapter and throughout the course: reading for meaning and reading like a writer. It is worth spending quite a bit of time on this section, as many of the issues it raises will be new to most students. The section begins with a brief illustration of annotation, the activity which enables the reading strategies students will be using. The section then walks students through a critical reading of a complete sample essay. For class activities to be used in conjunction with this section, see Part 5 of this instructor's manual.

The sample essay provided for these exercises, a piece by Audre Lorde, clearly demonstrates the basic strategies used by autobiographical writers: telling the story, presenting scenes and people, and creating an autobiographical impression. The Reading like a Writer section following the essay will break these down into more specific strategies.

Reading for Meaning

The first set of questions and suggestions following the sample essay are designed to help students focus closely on the text, speculating about the significance of the event and clarifying their understanding of Audre Lorde's essay. A similar section follows each of the readings in the chapter. As students use these suggestions to make their own meaning, you can expect that students will find somewhat different meanings in the essay because their own experience and interests lead them to focus on different parts of it.

Reading like a Writer

This section helps students shift their focus from what happens in the story to how the writer tells the story—from reading exclusively as readers to reading as prospective writers. Students are introduced to four major strategies of autobiographical writing—*telling the story, describing the scene, describing a person,* and *conveying the autobiographical significance.* Through a series of brief critical reading and writing tasks, students focus on how Lorde uses each of these strategies. *Telling the story* is presented specifically in terms of shaping the story and pacing the story; sections on use of detail and point of view contribute to *describing the scene.* Strategies for *describing a person* include physical description, revealing personality and motive, and suggesting relationships, while *conveying the autobiographical significance* is discussed in terms of presenting the authorial persona and disclosing the autobiographical significance.

While the Reading like a Writer section following this sample essay presents a full range of strategies for autobiographical writing, corresponding sections following each of the subsequent readings in the chapter will focus more narrowly on one or two strategies particularly appropriate to the analysis of each essay.

Telling the Story: Shaping and Pacing. Students may note that Lorde's narrative does not reach the specific afternoon of the event until paragraph 13—more than halfway through the essay—and that the story does not reach its climax until paragraph 18, just two paragraphs before the end. Students should also note that the simple chronological narrative leading up to the event is interrupted in several places by Lorde's reflections—from both her adolescent and her later adult perspectives—on American racism and her parents' response to it. The "action" of the story is also briefly slowed by the richly detailed list of foods in paragraph 4. When you discuss students' responses to this task, you might encourage them to speculate about how Lorde's essay would have been different if her narrative had led quickly and directly to the central event, leaving the more reflective material until after the climax of the action.

This task should help students recognize the function of Lorde's deliberate interruptions of her narrative in building tension or suspense. You may find that while some students find these interruptions contribute to the sense of mounting tension, other students may find these passages—particularly a lengthy reflective passage such as paragraph 7—distracting.

Describing the Scene: Detail and Point of View. This task asks students to look closely at the descriptive passages of Lorde's essay. They may be surprised by the distribution of details in Lorde's descriptions: she focuses very little on the sights and sounds of Washington, D.C., which might have been expected to loom larger in a young visitor's memory. Instead, she uses the most detail in her descriptions of the two food-related scenes, "bracketing" the central event with contrasting descriptions of atmosphere, from the warmth and comfort of the train scene to the atmosphere in the ice cream parlor which shifts from pleasantly cool to icy and hostile.

Students might also note that Lorde uses a variety of points of view—fixed and moving, close up and distant. In the train, the scene is observed close up; some students may suggest that, while the point of view is essentially fixed, the scene also suggests movement, a sense of excitement. This excitement is dimmed and the point of view becomes more distant on the streets of Washington, D.C.—a distance imposed by the writer's vision problem but also by her increasing discomfort and sense of alienation. Finally, her excitement is extinguished altogether in the ice cream parlor, and the point of view is fixed almost to paralysis until indignation takes over.

Describing People: Providing Physical Description, Revealing Personality, and Suggesting Relationships. This activity has several functions. By helping students focus on the very specific *purpose* of Lorde's physical description, this task should help students anticipate a common pitfall for inexperienced writers of autobiography: the tendency to include too much physical description, creating a police-blotter effect without contributing to the story.

In addition, this task should help students see that most autobiographical writers rely on a combination of strategies to reveal the personalities of characters in their stories, both telling the reader directly about people and "showing" the reader the people through their own words and actions. Students should also consider Lorde's purpose in this essay, and how the essay might have been different if her purpose had been to create a fully developed portrait of either or both of her parents.

As Lorde's parents play a central role in her first encounters with racism, students should note that Lorde's attitude toward her parents is neither wholly positive nor wholly negative; instead, her portrayal reflects an ambivalence appropriate to the complexity of her family relationships and the situation they are in. This concept of ambivalence may help students avoid the tendency in their own writing to either condemn or idealize their subjects.

Conveying the Autobiographical Significance. This task helps students compare the writer's past perspective at the time of the event with her later perspective at the time of writing. Students may note that, while both the young and the later Lorde are critical not only of racism but of her parents' attitude toward it, the somewhat naive indignation of the earlier perspective becomes a deeper, more informed bitterness in the writer's later perspective.

Students should have little trouble discerning that the significance of this event is that the trip to Washington, D.C., serves not as a "reward" for Lorde but as an abrupt introduction to the realities of racism. Students might refer to their responses to the previous task to examine how this significance has deepened as the writer has matured. Some students may note Lorde's use of her vision problem as a kind of metaphor for the pain of having one's eyes rudely opened.

RESOURCES FOR TEACHING THE READINGS

The reading selections in this chapter, beginning with the sample essay described above, represent the major types of autobiographical subjects: remembered incidents, phases, people, and places. Like Audre Lorde, Annie Dillard and Russell Baker focus on single incidents in their child- or young adulthoods. The next selection, by Itabari Njeri, treats an extended and significant phase of the author's life. The fourth selection, Laurie Abraham's portrait of her father after her parents' divorce, focuses on a person. The final selection is by a student, Brad Benioff, recounting how he and his water polo coach won each other's respect.

These selections cover a variety of subjects and reveal a range of strategies and approaches to these subjects. Students can learn from these diverse essays that autobiographical writing addresses many topics—some humorous, some painful—tells about them in an engaging way, describes them vividly so that readers can imagine them, and explains their significance in the writers' lives. Students can also see that autobiographical writing contains self-disclosure, and that readers are attracted by writers' willingness to share personal information.

The material that follows introduces each reading selection and offers some suggestions for engaging students with the sections on reading for meaning and reading like a writer and the ideas for writing following each reading.

Annie Dillard, **A Chase**

This selection is an example of the narration of a single incident from the autobiographer's childhood. Although the incident is brief and seemingly mundane, Dillard clearly considers it important; this selection should help students see how real autobiographical significance can be located in the most ordinary of events.

Reading for Meaning

This section encourages students to read and reread the essay closely, beginning with some speculations about what Dillard wants her readers to undertand. Starting with the author's reasons for writing about a specific incident ensures that as students explore meaning, they will stay closer to the text. Speculating about purpose requires thinking about the fundamental "why" of a text. Then students can go on to explore any meanings that interest them. For the first reading in each chapter, we suggest that you lead your class through this activity, helping students understand how the activity works and reminding them of the important roles of rereading and annotating in making meaning from a text before inviting them to write on their own in response to the activity. Also, especially after this first reading selection in the chapter, you might want to collect students' writing in response to this activity, going over it quickly to see how thoroughly students are exploring the meaning of the text. You could also read a few of the more interesting responses aloud in class.

Extending Meaning through Conversation. This section also introduces a new feature in the fourth edition of *Reading Critically, Writing Well*: a group activity called Extending Meaning through Conversation in which students discuss, with one or two other students, their possibly differing impressions of the meaning of Dillard's story. Through corresponding activities following each reading selection, as well as the more general collaborative activities that open each assignment chapter, students should become increasingly conscious of important issues of purpose and audience. If you are beginning your course with this chapter, you might set aside some class time following this activity to discuss how it went and what meanings seemed to emerge in conversation.

Reading like a Writer: Telling a Story Dramatically

This section highlights word choice, and particularly the choice of verbs—an element often overlooked by inexperienced readers but very useful to the writer of autobiography. In the crucial "chase" scene, students are asked to focus on the verbs Dillard chooses.

Students should note that Dillard chooses verbs that are interesting and appropriately dramatic—*choking, pounding, fling, aim, dive*—and should note the role these "action verbs" play in heightening the drama of the narrative. Astute students may also notice that the variety of Dillard's sentence length and structure serves not only to vary the rhythm of her writing, but also to enhance the drama: the sense of tension generated in the short, choppy sentences of paragraph 11 is released in the long, complex sentences of paragraphs 12, 13, and 14, for instance.

Considering Ideas for Your Own Writing

This section helps students begin to consider possible topics for their own autobiographical essays, and to anticipate some of the challenges specific to particular types of topics. A corresponding section follows each reading selection in the chapter. If students write out their ideas for writing, then they can try them out in class and you can begin to help them think through the issues involved in choosing an autobiographical topic.

Russell Baker, **Smooth and Easy**

Baker tells a fast-paced amusing narrative about failure and success. In our introduction to this selection, we ask students to notice how Baker uses humor in writing about an experience that probably didn't seem funny at the time. Baker has so much emotional and temporal distance from this event that he can emphasize the humorous aspects of what must have been an ordeal for him. The autobiographical significance is located in the paradox that he had to lose control of himself before he could gain control of the aircraft; he had to accept failure in order to succeed. In this selection, students see a writer telling a funny, revealing story about himself. They see that autobiographical writing need not be solemn or earnest to be successful.

Reading for Meaning

We invite students to reread Baker's essay as more than merely an amusing story by focusing on complex underlying issues and attitudes. Again, though, here they choose what to write about, what meanings to explore. If one of our suggestions for making meaning seems especially important to you, however, you could lead a class discussion about it or ask students to discuss it in small groups.

Extending Meaning through Conversation. Students are also invited to develop their understanding of Baker's story by discussing it with one or two classmates. Students may find that their reactions to this essay vary broadly; some will see it as a charming and lighthearted "coming of age" story, while others may perceive disturbing undertones in the attitudes Baker's essay represents toward war, women, and drinking. You could follow up briefly on this activity by talking in class about how these differences among the meanings made by different readers are natural and even useful.

Contextualizing (A Further Strategy for Reading for Meaning). Before students attempt this exercise, have them see the section on contextualizing in Appendix 1, A Catalog of Critical Reading Strategies. There students will find a demonstration of this strategy in use. Periodically throughout assignment Chapters 2–9, we refer students to this catalog. Following selected readings in each chapter, students are asked to complete a critical reading task in addition to Reading for Meaning and Reading like a Writer, thus ensuring that they gain extensive practice with a broad range of strategies.

In this case, we introduce students to the important strategy of contextualizing. This task guides students through a reading of Baker's essay in its social and historical context. Students are asked to identify the values and attitudes underlying the text, and to compare and contrast these with their own sensibilities. This particular strategy is especially appropriate to the reading of Baker's essay. As students learn in the Reading like a Writer section following the piece, the suspense of the narrative depends in part on the extent to which the reader is able to empathize with the writer. Students whose immediate reaction to Baker's story was strongly negative will find themselves more likely to empathize with Baker when they understand that he is writing out of a particular social and historical situation.

Reading like a Writer: Describing People

This task serves two functions. It should help students to see that physical description need not be lengthy to be effective, and that, in fact, the carefully chosen small detail, such as Total Loss Smith's "movie killer" lips, may be more dramatically revealing of character than the most thorough physical portrait. In addition, this exercise should help students begin to recognize the importance of dialogue in presenting people.

Compare. This feature, new to the fourth edition of *Reading Critically, Writing Well*, appears after one or two reading selections in each chapter. By encouraging students to complete this activity, you can help them not only to make basic connections between and among the readings, identifying both similarities and differences, but also to become increasingly aware of the full range of strategies available to writers in each genre. In this case, students should note that both Baker and Dillard are quite selective in their choice of details in describing people. As novice writers of autobiography may tend to over-describe the people in their stories, presenting large chunks of description which interrupt the narrative of their essays, this is an important activity.

Considering Ideas for Your Own Writing

This section invites students to consider writing about an event similar to the one in the selection they have just read. The questions highlight the issue of past versus present perspective, asking students to consider whether they have enough emotional distance from the events about which they may write.

Itabari Njeri, Land of the Doo-Wops

Unlike the previous reading selections in this chapter which focus on specific incidents or events, Njeri's piece treats an entire phase of her life during which she was led to reevaluate her abilities and aspirations, and to make a major change in her career and life goals. In the introduction to this selection, students are asked to consider not only what they learn about Njeri from reading her story, but also what Njeri might have learned about herself in writing it—an important reminder of the effects of autobiographical writing not only on the reader but on the writer.

Reading for Meaning

Students are invited to focus on the autobiographical significance of this phase in Njeri's life, examining the differences between Njeri's past and present perspectives as well as the differences between her musical training and the "real world" of music as a business.

Extending Meaning through Conversation. Once again, we invite students to explore their understanding of the selection by discussing it with one or two other students. Because Njeri's essay at least implicitly points to provocative issues of race and gender, you may find that students will bring a wide range of meanings to their discussion; in order to ensure that their conversations remain focused on the text itself, you might find it useful to circulate among pairs or groups.

Reading like a Writer: Presenting a Phase through Anecdotes

Students will need to recognize the differences between writing about an event and writing about a longer phase. This section should help them focus on the decisions Njeri makes regarding precisely which incidents to select for her narrative. Students' attention is also drawn to the transitions Njeri uses between incidents.

Considering Ideas for Your Own Writing

This section asks students to consider writing about phases in their own lives during which they were involved in new or challenging activities. Students are invited to reflect on the people and incidents involved in these phases of their lives.

Laurie Abraham, Divorced Father

While the writers of the previous selections focus on specific events or phases, Abraham's piece illustrates a third option for writers of autobiography: a significant person in the writer's life, in this case, her father.

Reading for Meaning

Once again, this section offers students suggestions for enriching their understanding of the meaning of Abraham's story, beginning with general guidelines for reflection on the selection, and concluding with specific ideas for developing an understanding of Abraham's relationship with her father. Although we do not invite students here to relate the essay to their personal experiences, you may find that many students have strong feelings about parent-child relationships and about divorce. If students are using their personal experience to make meaning from the text, you might invite them to do so orally in class, being sure that they do not move entriely away from the text itself. You can help them make explicit connections between their experience and the text.

Extending Meaning through Conversation. Students are also invited to discuss the meanings they have constructed on their own with one or two of their classmates. Once again, because students may be bringing their own experience to bear heavily on their undertandings of this selection, you might want to help them stay on track by moving from group to group.

Reading like a Writer: Describing a Person through Anecdotes and Recurring Activities

This section alerts students to the fact that autobiographical writers often choose both one-time and recurring incidents to create revealing portraits of people they have known over a long period of time. Students should note how the balance of specific anecdotes and recurring events helps Abraham convey not only a portrait of her father, but also a sense of the autobiographical significance of their relationship.

Considering Ideas for Your Own Writing

This section reminds students that, especially in writing about people they have known over long periods of time, they will need to consider carefully their selection of both anecdotes and recurring activities in presenting their subjects.

Brad Benioff, **Rick**

Benioff shows how his relationship with Rick developed over a short period of time, and what he learned about himself as a result of it. Like the preceding selection by Laurie Abraham, his essay is therefore about a phase in his life, as well as about a person.

Reading for Meaning

Here we remind students that autobiographical essays about remembered people are primarily essays about *relationships*. Students are invited to focus on what we learn not only about the subject of the essay but about the writer himself in this selection.

Extending Meaning through Conversation. Their impressions of the autobiographical significance of Benioff's story should provide interesting material for discussion with other students in this activity. While some students will find Benioff's essay a successful example of writing in this genre, others may find it somewhat predictable and heavy-handed.

Reading like a Writer: Describing a Person through Visual Details and Dialogue

This section asks students to focus specifically on the strategies writers use in presenting people: through physical description and through actions and words. If you have time to preview this activity, you might refer students back to the strategies for presenting people discussed in the Reading like a Writer section following the sample essay by Audre Lorde, and also to the corresponding section following Russell Baker's piece.

Writing up the results of their analysis, students should note that Benioff uses physical description fairly sparingly, concentrating it primarily at his own first sight of his subject in paragraph 6. (Students may differ over whether Benioff's repetitive sentence structure in this paragraph is deliberate or merely clumsy.) He later echoes specific details of his coach's appearance, using the coach's trademark dark glasses, which he removes only at the end of the essay, to signify the change in his relationship to his subject. Students will have no problem seeing that Benioff moves from using details that create a negative, almost sinister impression in his initial description to using details in the conclusion (the smile, the handshake) to create a positive, friendly impression. More sophisticated readers may find the abrupt about-face in the coach's attitude at once predictable and unconvincing. Students should also note Benioff's use of dialogue (or, before the coach's change in attitude, monologue) and how this contributes to his characterization of his subject.

Compare. This activity helps students focus on two important strategies writers of autobiography use in presenting people: visual description and dialogue. Comparing Benioff's essay with the previous selection by Laurie Abraham should help students gain a sense of the options open to them as they plan their own autobiographical essays.

Reading like a Writer: A Follow-up Activity

Once students have completed the Reading like a Writer activities in each chapter, they will have produced a substantial amount of writing about what they have learned about each genre. You might encourage them at this point to review all the writing they have done, and to select one piece to revise and expand through further analysis. They would turn this in with their essay packages, or with their end-of-course portfolios.

Considering Ideas for Your Own Writing

Many students have had experiences similar to Benioff's, in which a particular adult has won their respect, perhaps after some initial conflict. The strength of Benioff's essay lies in the suspense generated by the tension between him and Rick. If your students have not had such difficulties with the person they want to write about, they will need to find something else in the relationship that they did not expect, or that made it memorable. Remind students that even though this kind of writing focuses on another person, it is still autobiographical and should therefore reveal something about the writer as well as the subject. It is best not to let students write about people they have met only recently, or with whom they are still in disagreement. Students can seldom achieve the necessary emotional distance from such subjects to recognize their autobiographical significance.

THINKING ABOUT WHAT MAKES AUTOBIOGRAPHY EFFECTIVE

This section, new in the fourth edition of *Reading Critically, Writing Well*, helps students focus on important strategies of autobiographical writing by rereading one selection from the chapter, either alone or with a small group, and by writing briefly about how the writer in question fulfills the basic features of successful autobiographical writing. This important new activity enables students to review and consolidate what they have learned about the genre of autobiography before they attempt to write in this genre themselves.

A GUIDE TO AUTOBIOGRAPHICAL WRITING

The guide leads students through a composing process that follows these stages:

Invention
>Finding an Autobiographical Topic
>Probing Your Topic
>>Recalling First Impressions
>>Exploring Your Present Perspective
>>Discovering Autobiographical Significance
>>>Learning More about Your Readers: A Collaborative Activity
>>Detailing the Scene
>>Reconstructing Dialogue
>>Restating Autobiographical Significance

Drafting
>Setting Goals
>Planning Your Draft
>Beginning
>Choosing Relevant Details

Reading a Draft Critically
>Reading for a First Impression
>Reading to Analyze
>>Telling the Story
>>Describing the Scene
>>Describing People
>>Conveying the Autobiographical Significance

Revising
>Revising to Tell the Story
>Describing the Scene
>Describing a Person
>Conveying the Autobiographical Significance
Reflecting on What You Have Learned about Writing Autobiography

In order to represent an incident or person vividly, students will need to generate many concrete details. You may need to encourage students to complete this invention activity fully and thoughtfully, pointing out that, although they are unlikely to use all of the details they generate during the invention sequence in their actual essays, it will be to their benefit to have a rich wealth of details from which to choose as they draft their own essays.

Whether they are writing about an event, phase, or person, many students tend to opt for the simplest structure—a chronological sequence—without stopping to consider alternatives. A chronological structure is quite acceptable (and most of the selections in this chapter follow this order) but students should realize that they need not begin their stories at the beginning and follow them all the way through to the end. A simple variation, for instance, is to begin the essay by engaging readers with some dialogue or action, or with a patch of vivid description, before filling in the context. And even if they do choose to follow a strict chronological

48

sequence, students should remember that they can control the pace of the narrative, slowing down to present the important parts in detail and summarizing the less important parts. In their first drafts, students often spend too much time on less significant, preliminary incidents, and not enough time on the most important moments.

SPECIAL PROBLEMS OF THIS WRITING ASSIGNMENT. We have noticed that students facing this assignment for the first time may have problems developing a well-paced, dramatic narrative and achieving the self-disclosure necessary to reveal the significance of the event, person, or phase.

In their first drafts of autobiographical essays, student writers tend to draw on what they know of storytelling conventions. Typically, this involves beginning with a general introduction, setting the scene or declaring the significance of the subject in broad terms. The succession of events is then played out in the body of the paper without much alteration in pace to include descriptive details, the writer's feelings at the time, and reflections with hindsight. A writer often forgets to show rather than to tell, to bring an experience alive with sensory detail rather than merely to record the sequence of events.

Many writers have initial difficulties managing the pace of a narrative, not realizing that the climax of an event can easily be undercut if pages of incidental events have misdirected readers' expectations. We find it useful to spend some time explaining ways to adjust the flow of time and control suspense. The readings offer good examples of how writers can do this.

For many writers, the companion to the convention of beginning a story with a general introduction is the convention of ending it with a moral. Unused to probing the personal significance of events, people, or phases they write about, inexperienced writers tend to translate this convention into a moralistic conclusion. Again we use the readings to point out ways in which reflection on the significance of an event, a person, or a phase can be woven into the narrative.

Self-disclosure does not come naturally to many students, and we find they need a good deal of encouragement and reassurance, particularly if the topic is a sensitive one. Often they go no further than to say that an event was very frightening or great fun, or that a person was wonderful or terrible. We encourage them to go deeper, to look at reasons for their actions and reactions. We find that few students explore the humorous or absurd possibilities of their topics and the personal insights that these can provide.

PROMISING AND UNPROMISING TOPICS. The writing assignment in this chapter gives students a wide choice of topics. This choice, as students soon discover, presents problems as well as opportunities. The chief problem comes when students choose subjects from which they do not have enough emotional distance.

When asked to choose a significant event, person, or phase, students frequently want to write about the first topic that comes to mind, often a recent experience or a traumatic one. An event that happened very recently may only appear to be important because it is on the writer's mind. While writing about such an event will help the writer understand it, the event may turn out not to have much meaning after all.

Traumatic events may also be problematic as topics, not because they lack significance but because they are too meaningful. Writing about a traumatic event may involve more self-disclosure than seems appropriate given the writing situation. On the other hand, the student may decide that writing about a traumatic event such as the death of a loved one can be therapeutic.

Looking back over the events and phases of their lives, as well as people they have known, for possible topics, writers understandably tend to think big. Major emotional landmarks readily suggest themselves: graduation, making the team, having an accident, failing the big test.

Some of these peak experiences represent initiations or rites of passage. They are prominent in the minds of many students and can make excellent autobiographical topics. A problem with these topics, however, is that many of them are common experiences, familiar to almost everyone. The challenge in writing about such a subject is to avoid the cliché, to find something unusual in the experience, or to give readers a new perspective on it. We encourage students to think twice before writing about their first experience on the ski slopes, the prom that was not all it promised to be, the event that would have embarrassed anyone. Experiences that exactly match expectations contain nothing surprising for readers, no new insights about themselves or discoveries about human nature. Students would do better to look beyond the obvious and consider some of the subtler experiences they may have had—moments of intense awareness, realizations, important changes that took place within themselves.

Chapter 3 OBSERVATION

The selections in this chapter are closely related to those in the preceding and following chapters. The discussion of Chapter 5 in this manual will cover some differences between observational, reflective, and explanatory writing. Here we would like to point out a few of the key differences between observational and autobiographical writing.

Whereas autobiographical writing attempts to find personal meaning in experience, and to transmit this meaning to readers through vivid storytelling, observational writing aims to present what writers have discovered about a subject outside of themselves by investigating it personally. Informing readers in a vivid, engaging way is the main purpose of observational writing.

WRITING ASSIGNMENT: Observation
Here is the writing assignment that appears near the beginning of Chapter 3:

> Write an observational essay about an intriguing person, place, or activity in your community. Your essay may be a brief profile of an individual based on one or two interviews; a description of a place or activity observed once or twice; or a longer, more fully developed profile of a person, place, or activity observed once or twice; or a longer, more fully developed profile of a person, place, or activity based on several observational visits and interviews conducted over several weeks.
>
> Observe your subject closely, and then present what you have learned in a way that both informs and engages readers.

Possible topic ideas follow each reading selection in a special section called Considering Ideas for Your Own Writing. A general list of topics is also included as part of the Invention section in the Guide to Observational Writing.

Observational Writing Situations

The situations that open this chapter suggest some of the possibilities for this kind of writing. Students can see right away that a profile may focus on a place (radio station), a person (scientist, artist), or an activity (urban renewal project). But they also see that these categories overlap: writing about a place involves presenting personalities and their activities; writing about a person involves describing his or her activities and the places in which they occur. Finally, these situations show that observational writing generally emphasizes the incongruous or unexpected, centering on the contrast between expectation and reality (the personal discovery about a radio station, for instance). Sometimes a controversy is uncovered (as in the case of the urban renewal project), while sometimes what is revealed is simply a fascinating observation, such as mural painting.

Practicing Observation: A Collaborative Activity

This group activity enables students to explore the rhetorical situation of the profile and prepares them to reflect on what they have learned. In Part 1, as they try out an idea with two or three fellow students, they become aware of what may interest readers. Then they step back in Part 2 to reflect on what they have learned. Because students find this activity so engaging, you will need to remind them to shift from telling about their subjects in Part 1 to discussing the rhetorical situation in Part 2.

A GUIDE TO READING OBSERVATIONAL WRITING

In this section, students are asked to read on two different levels: as readers and as writers. For class activities to use in conjunction with this section, see Part 5 of this manual.

Here, following a brief illustration of annotation, students are introduced to a sample essay—a selection from *Among School Children*, by Tracy Kidder. Students will want to note that, while Kidder's project is clearly to profile one person, teacher Chris Zajac, he relies on observations of activities, a place, and—especially—other people in presenting his profile.

Reading for Meaning

This section helps students develop meaning from the text by rereading it and by considering it in light of their personal knowledge and experience. You might want to have a few students share their responses in class as a way of encouraging a broader discussion of the meaning of the piece.

Reading like a Writer

Here, students are asked to shift their focus from the meaning of the essay to the specific strategies the writer uses to make meaning. These strategies fall into the broad categories of *detailing the scene and people, organizing the observations, engaging and informing readers,* and *conveying an impression of the subject.* In the critical reading and writing tasks that follow, each of these strategies is focused on more narrowly: *detailing the scene and people* focuses on ways in which writers of observation offer vivid presentations of their subjects, while *organizing the observations* draws students' attention toward methods of providing tension and drama through narrative or other methods of organization. (Both of these strategies should be familiar to students from the previous assignment in autobiographical writing.) *Engaging and informing readers* helps students see how writers engage and sustain readers' interest by presenting information in entertaining ways. *Conveying an impression of the subject* is discussed in terms of expressing an attitude toward the subject and conveying an interpretation or theme.

Detailing the Scene and People. Especially if they've just completed the autobiographical assignment presented in Chapter 2, students are likely to notice immediately that Kidder goes well beyond the visual in describing Zajac's classroom, incorporating a range of sounds, smells, and tactile sensations. Most students will find Kidder's characterizations of students and of Zajac herself both economical and effective; likewise, students will probably find that Kidder's presentation of the elementary classroom scene evokes a universal experience. In their written responses to this task, students should probably be able to comment on the importance of careful selection of detail in Kidder's presentation of scene and people.

Organizing the Observations. Students will learn in this chapter that writers of observation often use a narrative framework, as Kidder does, to organize their observations. If your students have worked with the previous chapter, Chapter 2: Autobiography, they should be familiar with the strategies by which writers shape and pace their narratives. If you have not used Chapter 2, or if you feel students need a review of these strategies, you might find it useful to walk students through the essay, helping them to notice that Kidder manipulates his narration to replicate the transition from drowsiness to excitement experienced by Zajac's students. You might point out, for instance, that the pace of the narrative picks up dramatically at the end of paragraph 4, where Zajac decides to surprise her students by reversing her role with theirs.

Engaging and Informing Readers. Students will immediately notice the specificity with which Kidder's selection begins, drawing readers into a particular and very likely familiar scene. Through careful use of narrative strategies, students should note, Kidder is able to capture the interest of his readers. Students should also see that Kidder inserts diverse information—gathered over a long period of prior observation of and interviews with his subject—into his narrative.

Conveying an Impression of the Subject. Students may need to be reminded that observational writing rarely involves a simple, neutral presentation of a subject: in most cases, writers exhibit a distinct attitude toward their subjects. While Kidder, like most observational writers, comes across as being somewhat detached, he clearly admires Chris Zajac as a teacher and is, at least occasionally, amused by her interactions with her students.

In addition to expressing their attitudes toward their subjects, observational writers generally attempt to present an interpretation or evaluation of their topics. In this sense, this assignment provides an opportunity to preview assignments in which students will be asked to defend a point of view, detailed in later chapters in the text.

Although this task may seem simple, it helps students bring together the strategies for successful observational writing discussed so far: keeping in mind the attitude and interpretation they've discussed in the two previous sections, and their examinations of the way Kidder details scenes and people from the first task, students will note that all of these elements are interrelated. Each detail is carefully selected to contribute to Kidder's implicit interpretation of his subject.

RESOURCES FOR TEACHING THE READINGS

This chapter presents a variety of examples of observational writing. The first essay, by an unidentified staff writer of the *New Yorker*, describes the extraordinary soup kitchen of Mr. Albert Yeganeh. The second reading, Lisa Jones's *Girls on the Strip*, profiles African-American comic-strip artist Barbara Brandon. *Bull Riding School*, by Jane and Michael Stern, offers an account of the unusual and colorful curriculum of the school named in the title. John McPhee's *The New York Pickpocket Academy* gives a sharply focused profile of pickpockets who frequent a farmer's market in Brooklyn. The rich details of people and activities and the immediacy of the profile is in part a consequence of McPhee's decision to present his observations from his point of view as a worker in the market. The final essay, *Dead Air*, by college student Craig Elsten, profiles a college radio station.

The readings in this chapter illustrate various kinds of observational writing: profiles of people, places, and events. By reading and analyzing these selections, students will discover that good observational writing is generally characterized by a specific subject and a main point or interpretation, a vivid description of the subject so that readers can imagine what the writer observed, and a clear organization so that readers can follow the essay easily.

The following material introduces each reading and explores the possibilities of the sections on reading for meaning and reading like a writer and the ideas for writing that follow each reading.

The New Yorker, Soup

Two things are quickly noticeable in this portrait of Albert Yeganeh and his soup kitchen. The first is that the writer introduces the essay with a long monologue by Mr. Yeganeh. Most observational essays, especially short ones, would summarize or break up such a long speech. The second thing most readers notice is the writer's decision to organize the essay by presenting a strong character portrait of Mr. Yeganeh and then by shifting to a point of view that makes readers feel as if they are approaching Mr. Yeganeh's soup kitchen for the first time.

Reading for Meaning
This section asks students to consider the writer's purpose in writing about Mr. Yeganeh's soup kitchen, and about the writer's attitude toward his or her subject. Students are encouraged to annotate as they read and reread the essay; you might remind them of the importance of this critical reading strategy by referring them back to the sample of annotation that opens A Guide to Reading Observational Writing. The section also encourages students to connect their own experiences and attitudes directly to the text of the essay. Especially as this is the first reading in the chapter, you might collect and quickly skim students' writing for this activity, making sure students are on track and perhaps reading aloud a few of the more thoughtful responses.

Extending Meaning through Conversation. This section, a corresponding version of which follows each of the readings in the text, invites students to develop their understanding of the meaning of this selection by discussing it in pairs or small groups, with particular attention to differences among student perceptions of the piece. While many students will find Mr. Yeganeh a colorful and somewhat charming character, for instance, others may find his approach a bit abrasive. You may find it helpful to move among pairs or groups of students as they discuss the essay, offering suggestions and helping groups stay focused on the reading. As usual, especially with the first reading in each chapter, you may want to set aside some class time so that students can share the results of this activity with you and the class as a whole.

Reading like a Writer: Detailing the Scene and People

This section asks students to analyze several paragraphs of the essay closely, looking for the details the writer has selected in presenting Mr. Yeganeh and his soup kitchen. As they write briefly based on their analyses, students should be able to report that the physical details do more than simply describe the scene and people: they also contribute to the writer's portrait of Mr. Yeganeh by revealing his attitudes toward his customers (paragraph 4) and his interactions with his employees (paragraph 5) and customers (paragraphs 7–10). Once again, for the first reading in the chapter, you might lead your students through the analysis as a group, guiding them in a thorough analysis of the paragraphs. This is a useful opportunity to remind students of the importance of rereading, annotating, and note-taking in reading critically. Once students have completed the writing activity, you could ask a few of them to share their responses in class.

Considering Ideas for Your Own Writing

With our students, unusual places on campus or in the community are favorite subjects for the observational essay assignment. Help your students consider the implications of their choices: how they would go about observing the place, when they would observe, whom they would interview, from what vantage point would they observe, and so on. Help them imagine themselves carrying through with the entire assignment; encourage them to think like writers at work.

Lisa Jones, **Girls on the Strip**

As the introductory material to this selection points out, Jones's essay differs from the previous selection in two important ways: it focuses less on a particular person than on that person's work, and it more distinctly foregrounds the role of the observational writer herself. As students begin to plan their own observational writing, they will want to consider the options suggested by these differences. The introduction to the piece also reminds students that writing in this genre need not be formal, but that, in fact, observational writers often achieve their effects through direct, lively language, and, sometimes, through references to their own experiences.

Reading for Meaning

Like the introductory material, this section begins by drawing students' attention to the author's personal connection with her subject, providing a useful starting point from which students can expand on their impressions of the meaning of the selection.

Extending Meaning through Conversation. In this activity, students are once again invited to share their perceptions of the essay in small groups. As Jones's piece goes beyond a simple portrait of an artist to touch on deeper issues of race and gender, this activity should elicit some interesting discussion; you might provide some class time following this activity for students to share their responses with you and the larger group.

Reading like a Writer: Engaging and Informing Readers

One challenge that students will face as they proceed with their own observational writing projects is how to present background information while keeping readers' interest engaged. While the information presented in Jones's profile of Barbara Brandon is by no means dry or technical, the writer has nevertheless carefully considered its placement within the essay. Students should already have noticed that, as in the sample essay by Tracy Kidder, Jones's firsthand observation of Brandon and her work—much of it presented through lively quotations—is interspersed with background information about Brandon's career and about "black comic strip history." Once students have analyzed and written briefly about this aspect of Brandon's essay, you might give them time to compare their responses in pairs or small groups, and then allow them a few minutes to add to their own writing what insights they have gained.

Considering Ideas for Your Own Writing

This section invites students to consider writing about an entrepreneur of any variety, examining the challenges and rewards of such work. Because this type of profile, like Jones's, is likely to be largely interview-based, we offer some specific suggestions for gathering material from profile subjects.

Jane and Michael Stern, **Bull Riding School**

As students compare this selection to previous readings in the chapter, they will probably notice that it contains more narrative action (especially in paragraphs 12-16) than the previous selection by Lisa Jones; they may also note that, while each of the previous essays, by Kidder, the anonymous *New Yorker* writer, and Jones, focus on single people, the Sterns also include brief but telling profiles of secondary characters: the students at Gary Leffew's bull-riding school. If your students have worked with Chapter 2: Autobiography, this selection provides a good opportunity to review strategies of both narration of action and description of people; if you have not used Chapter 2, this is a fine opportunity to introduce and reinforce students' understanding of these strategies.

Reading for Meaning

This activity encourages students to explore their impressions of the Sterns's essay, directing their attention to the authors' treatment of the school itself, the teacher, and the students. As students reread and annotate the essay, they should find their impressions of the Sterns's attitude toward their subject becoming clearer.

Extending Meaning through Conversation. Students may find that their views of this piece differ widely: while many will read this as a straightforward and colorful essay about an interesting topic, some students may perceive a certain amount of condescension on the part of the writers toward both Gary Leffew and his pupils, while others may be disturbed by the intimations of cruelty represented by the "electric prod" mentioned in paragraph 13. You might ask each pair or group of students to report to the class briefly on differences that remain after discussion, and you could talk to the class about the acceptability of differences among readers.

Exploring the Significance of Figurative Writing (A Further Strategy for Reading for Meaning). This supplemental activity calls students' attention to the role of figurative language, not only in creating a colorful profile but in in conveying the writers' attitudes toward their subject. Students are referred to Appendix 1, where this critical reading strategy is presented in more detail. Once students have completed this activity, you might ask them to share their findings briefly in class.

Reading like a Writer

The preceding exercise in exploring the figurative language in the essay should help students move smoothly into this activity, as the authors rely heavily on figurative language in detailing Gary Leffew, and, to a somewhat lesser extent, his students. In addition, students who have worked with Chapter 2: Autobiography will be familiar with many of the resources highlighted in this section, which are based on strategies of narration and description. We draw students' attention to specific paragraphs in which the writers draw upon a full range of resources in detailing their subject. Students are then asked to comment on how successful the writers have been in selecting details to provide a full and engaging profile.

Compare. In this activity, which follows one or two readings in each chapter, students are asked to go beyond their analysis and writing about a specific essay to compare and contrast the ways different writers in the chapter use the same strategies. This type of comparison helps students gain a broader sense of possible use of strategies within each genre, and it is such an important activity that you might want to lead the class through it, giving them time afterwards to reflect briefly in writing on the class discussion.

Considering Ideas for Your Own Writing

This section invites students to consider writing about a specialized class or training program, such as the bull riding school featured in the reading selection, and to refer to their own experience as they select such a topic. You might remind students that a topic of this type will probably demand quite a bit of planning, as observations may need to be arranged in advance.

John McPhee, **The New York Pickpocket Academy**

In this selection, McPhee describes scenes from a day in the Brooklyn farmers' market, where he observes the interactions between petty thieves and their victims. The accumulation of observed details is characteristic of McPhee's style. The selection offers little commentary, but readers can infer McPhee's purpose from the way he has selected and arranged his details and examples. The scenes and anecdotes speak for themselves. Another feature of the selection is McPhee's use of the present tense to convey the unfolding drama of a day in the market.

Reading for Meaning

In observational writing, where it can often seem to students that the writer is merely telling what he or she experienced, the main point may not be immediately apparent. However, students should realize that writers like McPhee make points about their subjects as they describe and narrate them, even though they rarely announce their points in thesis statements. Clearly, one of McPhee's purposes in this selection is to describe the extent of crime in the market. "Possibly Fifty-ninth Street is the New York Pickpocket Academy," he remarks, and he provides plenty of supporting evidence for this observation. However, he also seems to be making the point that altruism and honesty occasionally appear even amid so much crime and are appreciated by those who benefit from them. McPhee's purpose seems to be to present a complex view of the market and the different impulses demonstrated by people who work, shop, and steal there every day.

Extending Meaning through Conversation. Once again, students are invited to develop their understanding of the essay by discussing it with one or two other students. You could give students a few minutes following this activity to extend their own notes on the reading, adding any insights they have gleaned from their discussion.

Reading like a Writer: Organizing the Observations

As they plan and write their own observational essays, one of the most important decisions students will make is whether to organize their material narratively or topically. Drawing students' attention to the fact that, unlike the earlier selections in this chapter, McPhee's profile is organized around a narrative framework, we ask students to outline his essay carefully, using strategies which are further detailed in Appendix 1. Students are then asked to explore their findings briefly in writing.

Compare. This activity, which follows one or two readings in each chapter, should help students gain a sense of the possibilities open to writers in each genre. By examining the decisions made by two or more writers in each chapter, students will be better prepared to begin making the same types of decisions as they begin their own essays. In this case, students will find it especially interesting to speculate about how McPhee's essay would have been different if he had presented his material topically, and how "Soup" or "Bull Riding School" might have been different if their writers had relied more heavily on narrative in presenting their observations.

Considering Ideas for Your Own Writing

We ask students to consider writing their own observational essays about large public places, filled with people and action. While these types of topics offer rich material for writers of observation, you might remind students that they will face the challenge of limiting and focusing their observations, as McPhee does. As usual, part of the point of this activity is to connect students' task as writers immediately to what they have learned as readers.

Craig Elsten, **Dead Air**

Elsten's essay about a radio station on the campus where he is a student helps students see that good topics for observational essays can be found close to home, at their own schools or in their own communities.

Reading for Meaning

Students are asked to explore their understanding of Elsten's essay, commenting on the impression he seems to convey of KSDT. Students should also consider the extent to which Elsten's essay is successful in combining information and entertainment. As students reread and annotate the essay, they will be able to see how these basic features of observational writing function in Elsten's essay. Students are also invited to relate their own experiences to Elsten's observations. As many students may use their own job experiences to make meaning from this text, you might make sure that they aren't moving too far away from the text itself by inviting to share their stories in class, so that you can lead them back to the essay to make explicit connections between their experiences and the text.

Extending Meaning through Conversation. As students continue to explore and develop their understanding of the meaning of this piece by discussing it with one or two classmates, you might circulate from group to group, helping students stay focused on the text itself. Remind students that they can reread and annotate the text together as part of this activity.

Reading like a Writer: Conveying an Impression

While there will probably be some variety in the possible interpretations students impute to Elsten's essay, most will agree that his interpretation of his subject revolves around the curious phenomenon of a radio station to which almost no one is able to listen. Students should note that, in addition to his own commentary, Elsten allows the employees of KSDT to speak for themselves in support of his interpretation. Once students have completed these analyzing and writing activities, you might ask them to share their responses briefly in small groups or with the class.

Reading like a Writer: A Follow-up Activity

To help students continue to develop their understanding of observational writing, you might have them go back over the writing they have generated in response to the Reading like a Writer activities throughout the chapter. After reviewing their own writing, students could choose one piece to expand through further analysis and writing. You could have students turn this piece in with the essay package or in an end-of-course portfolio.

Considering Ideas for Your Own Writing

We find that this writing idea has special appeal for our students. There turn out to be many "scenes" on campus worth looking behind. How *does* the soccer team prepare for a game? How *is* the student newspaper or an academic journal produced? How *are* materials processed in a library archive? There are many possibilities. Help students imagine how they would go about developing a behind-the-scenes profile.

THINKING ABOUT WHAT YOU HAVE LEARNED ABOUT OBSERVATIONAL ESSAYS

As students prepare to begin their own essays, we find it especially important that they pause to consider and articulate what they have learned from the readings about the features of each genre. Students are asked to focus closely on the strategies used by writers of observation by choosing one essay from the chapter to analyze in more detail. After examining the author's (or authors') purpose and audience, we ask students to comment on how—and how well—the essay fulfills what we have identified following each reading as the basic features of successful observational writing. Concentrating on one essay at this point should help students to review, remember, and eventually use the observational writing strategies to which they've been exposed throughout the chapter. Whether you have students complete this activity individually or work in small groups with other students who have selected the same essay, you might give them the opportunity to share their ideas in class as a way of stimulating a productive discussion of the features of successful writing of this type. One way of doing this would be to outline the features of observational writing on the board, and then have students comment on how successfully each writer meets the challenges of each feature.

A GUIDE TO OBSERVATIONAL WRITING

The guide leads students through a composing process that follows these steps:

Invention
    Choosing a Subject
    Probing Your Subject
    Investigating Your Subject
        Visiting a Place
        Interviewing a Person
        Gathering Published Information
    Deciding on the Impression You Mean to Convey
    Analyzing Your Readers
        Learning More about Your Readers: A Collaborative Activity
Drafting
    Setting Goals
    Planning Your Draft
    Beginning
Reading a Draft Critically
    Reading for a First Impression
    Reading to Analyze
        Detailing the Scene and People
        Organizing the Observations
        Engaging and Informing Readers
        Conveying an Impression
Revising
    Revising to Detail the Scene and People
    Revising to Organize the Observations
    Revising to Engage and Inform Readers
    Revising to Convey an Impression of the Subject
    Reflecting on What You Have Learned about Observational Writing

Choosing a suitable topic is particularly important for this assignment because students will need to invest a good deal of their time visiting the place or person, conducting interviews, and/or doing firsthand research. If students are unable to think of a topic by sitting alone in their rooms with a blank sheet of paper or brainstorming with family and friends, you might be able to help them by suggesting some sources of topics: the business index at the back of the phone book is a ready-made list of potential profile topics ranging from jewelry designers to printing companies; a map of the area can reveal some potentially interesting places to investigate; local newspapers can be another source of inspiration. The main criteria for an observational writing topic are that it be personally interesting to the student, potentially interesting to readers, and accessible or researchable within the time available for the assignment.

Students may wonder why they need to do the exercises under Probing Your Subject with their topics. While not all the questions may be relevant for every student's topic, probing the subject helps students establish their preconceptions about the subject (which may contrast with what they later discover) and decide whether the topic seems interesting enough to pursue. This step in the invention sequence is a small investment of time that could save them the trouble of investigating less interesting topics.

As students do begin to investigate their topics, you will want to stress the importance of field research in observational writing: it is an essential part of the work students will do for this assignment. Depending on their subjects, students are likely to use both observation and interviews; most students will not have much experience with either. In Appendix 2: Strategies for Research and Documentation, we give students a detailed overview of strategies for these types of research. We lead students step by step through the observation and interview process, and, while some of this advice may seem like common sense (take a writing implement, prepare some interview questions in advance), students will find it useful. You might emphasize in particular the importance of reflecting on their observations and interviews immediately after the fact, reviewing and adding to their notes rather than relying on memory.

Students often have difficulty deciding on what impression they want to convey in their observational essays, so you may want to devote some class time to discussing the questions under this heading in the invention sequence. At this stage, the impression need only be a provisional one; reassure students that they can change it as they learn more about their subjects.

The next invention step is analyzing readers, and this is another stage at which students often need guidance, simply because few students are used to writing with any particular audience in mind aside from their instructor. You might want to specify a local newspaper or periodical that publishes observational articles, or you might let students identify the publication they would like to write for. The publication might be hypothetical, or you might insist that students write for an actual publication and encourage the most successful to submit their final typescripts to it. When analyzing their readers, then, students should describe the editors and readers of the publication, and perhaps the style of article that appears in it. We also invite students to analyze their readers further by briefly presenting potential subjects for their own observational essays in small groups; we find that hands-on, collaborative activities of this sort are especially useful in preparing students for the challenges they will face as they embark on their own essays.

When planning the organization of their essays, students often choose the easiest plan and merely organize information in the order in which they discovered it. Remind them that writers often organize their material according to a topical plan rather than a narrative. If students opt for a chronological sequence as their organizational principle, they should do so because that is a better plan than the alternatives, not because it is the only one they have considered. Likewise, remind students of the variety of beginnings demonstrated by the selections in this chapter, and tell them that they need not wait for the ideal beginning before they start drafting. Revision allows the beginning to be added later.

SPECIAL PROBLEMS OF THIS WRITING ASSIGNMENT. There are essentially two problems students have with this assignment. The first has to do with scheduling and the other with focusing. One of the best ways to focus an observational essay is to organize it around a dominant impression of the subject. By this we mean a unique or fresh perspective on a given subject, something that reveals a new or unexpected insight into that subject.

The scheduling problem arises from the difficulty many freshmen have in sustaining a long research project. In the guide to writing, we recommend that students establish their own research schedules. But we also suggest that you set up deadlines for various stages of the project—such as writing up notes on observational visits and interviews, preparing an outline, or writing the first draft—to help students keep on schedule. You could easily have students write up their observations and interviews and then use class time for peer workshops on these notes and write-ups.

Writing up their notes from observations and interviews and exchanging these write-ups with others in the class can also help students focus their observations. The focusing problem results from the overwhelming quantity of information students usually gather. The more they work with their material—analyzing it, writing about it, finding connections and patterns in it—the more cohesive their essays ultimately will be. As their drafts become more organized and cohesive, students will also be able to develop or discover the impressions they wish to convey in their essays.

PROMISING AND UNPROMISING TOPICS. Because the scope of this assignment is so broad, the opportunities for topics may seem so rich as to be inexhaustible. For many novice writers who have just arrived at a university (or a new city), the observational essay offers an ideal chance for exploration. Students should be encouraged to seek out unusual activities, people, or places. When you make the assignment, urge them to avoid topics with which they are overly familiar (for example, the summer job they have had for the last four years, their college dorm, etc.). If your students are writing a longer profile, they will need to pick a topic with plenty of activity, enough people for several interviews, and a circumscribed place that can be described specifically (profiles about "the beach" or "downtown" generally don't work, for instance).

Two other problems with selecting a topic are those of accessibility and security. Subjects that may sound exciting in theory may not be possible or appropriate in practice. A doctor or scientist may not be available for interviews; legal considerations might prevent a student from profiling an emergency room; a military installation or a nuclear power plant may be off-limits to the general public.

Similarly, you may want to discourage students from exploring topics that are potentially dangerous. It is natural, even commendable, for some people to want to do something a little daring, but it is not always a good idea. Students should think twice about profiling something like the county jail (which may be off-limits anyway), a place in a neighborhood with a high incidence of crime, or some activity that presents a health or safety hazard. On the one hand, you don't want your students to select mundane or drab topics, but on the other hand, you should urge them to use discretion when picking a subject to observe. All you really need to do is to encourage them to explore unfamiliar places or activities—the experience of discovery should be enough to yield a fresh and insightful angle. Part of the task, of course, is for students to get beneath the surface of whatever it is they are observing.

One way to involve all students in evaluating each other's topic choices is to circulate topic sheets. At the top of a sheet of paper students write a tentative title for their essays. Then they describe in two or three sentences the person, location, or activity that will be the subject of their profile. In one sentence, they identify possible readers (class members, readers of a particular newspaper or magazine, or perhaps a special group of readers with a need to know what the writer will discover). These sheets then circulate around the class, with students writing questions or comments, and even commenting on other students' comments.

We evaluate—approving, questioning, rejecting—students' topic choices for all our assignments. We evaluate the observational essay assignment most carefully of all because students are unlikely to have undertaken such a writing project and consequently cannot foresee the possibilities and problems of a topic.

Chapter 4 REFLECTION

What distinguishes the reflective essay, to borrow Virginia Woolf's words, is its "fierce attachment to an idea." In introducing this assignment, you might help students make connections between this assignment and the two previous assignments in the text: while autobiographers spin tales about significant events and people in their lives, and writers of observation present what they have discovered about a subject by investigating it personally, writers of reflection spin webs of ideas.

Reflective writing is a natural outgrowth of both autobiographical and observational writing. All three have their roots in personal experience, and all are concerned with the meaning or significance of that experience. But whereas autobiographers and most observational writers need only present their experience vividly to convey its significance, reflective writers must explore the meaning they find.

While autobiographers bring out personal significance, reflective writers, like writers of observation, look for general implications. Reflection stems from an observation or experience that raises a question or leads to an insight about the human situation. Reflective essayists write about the ways in which we live and interact with one another, the goals toward which we strive, and the shortcomings that hobble us. The reflective essay is typically a public meditation on what makes us human. The readings in this chapter, and the accompanying commentary and activities, should help students appreciate the value of this genre.

WRITING ASSIGNMENT: Reflection

Here is the writing assignment that appears near the beginning of Chapter 4:

Write a reflective essay based on something you experienced or observed. Describe it vividly so that readers can understand what happened and will care about what you have to say. In reflecting on what the particular occasion suggests, explore your own and society's attitudes and values. Reflective writing is like a conversation—you are writing not just for yourself but to share your thoughts with others, to stimulate their thinking as well as your own.

Possible topic ideas (Considering Ideas for Your Own Writing) follow each reading selection. A general list of topics is also included as part of the Invention section in the Guide to Reflective Writing.

Reflective Writing Situations

The three brief writing situations suggest a few of the possibilities for reflective writing. You could help your students notice that reflective writing takes place in both academic and non-academic settings, that it is written by both professional and nonprofessional writers, and that it has room alike for humor and for serious social commentary.

Practicing Reflection: A Collaborative Activity

This group activity enables students to imagine themselves as reflective writers, preparing them to approach the upcoming reading selections from a writer's perspective. As they try out ideas with two or three fellow students, they are reminded of the important dimensions of purpose and audience; then they step back to examine the rhetorical situation of writing a reflective essay. Because students are likely to get deeply involved in this activity, you may need to remind them to shift from their conversation about the occasion their group has chosen in part one to reflect more broadly on other considerations of the genre in part two.

A GUIDE TO READING REFLECTIVE WRITING

This section calls students' attention to the fact that they will be asked to read the upcoming selections from two different perspectives: that of readers, and that of writers of reflective essays. For class activities to use in conjunction with this section, see Part 5 of this manual.

Following a brief illustration of annotation, students are presented with a sample essay by Nicollette Toussaint entitled "Hearing the Sweetest Songs"—a reflection on her experiences with being "differently abled." Toussaint's essay is a good example of a short reflective essay, a meditation that explores and illustrates general ideas with concrete details.

Reading for Meaning

In this section, as in corresponding sections throughout the text, students are encouraged to focus closely on the content of the reading selection. Here, students are asked to respond to "Hearing the Sweetest Songs," beginning by considering the insights Toussaint provides into being disabled. Students are also invited to respond to Toussaint's reflections in light of their own experiences or observations, in addition to being offered several other suggestions for exploring the meaning of the essay.

Reading like a Writer

In this series of tasks, the focus shifts from the content and purpose of the essay to the specific strategies the reflective writer uses in achieving that purpose: *presenting the particular occasion, developing the reflections, maintaining topical coherence,* and *engaging readers.* In the following critical reading and writing tasks, each of these strategies is broken down more specifically. *Presenting the particular occasion* entails both narrating and describing, while *developing the reflections* takes place through asserting ideas, giving examples, posing questions, and comparing and contrasting. *Maintaining topical coherence* is discussed in terms of establishing a theme that connects all parts of a reflective essay. Students also learn that *engaging readers* involves the writer in presenting reflection vividly, perhaps in ways which surprise the reader. While the Reading like a Writer section following the sample essay provides a comprehensive catalog of these strategies, corresponding sections following each of the subsequent reading selections focus more narrowly on strategies particularly appropriate to the analysis of each essay. In each case, students will be asked to engage in a two-part activity including both analyzing and writing, following two of the readings in the chapter, they will also be invited to compare the ways in which two or more authors use specific strategies.

Presenting the Particular Occasion. We point out to students that Toussaint's essay begins not with a single particular occasion but with a pair of significantly related incidents. While Toussaint's narrative of these incidents is not as sustained, nor her description, perhaps, as detailed, as that of many of the writers in Chapter 2: Autobiography, and Chapter 3: Observation, students should nonetheless recognize many of these familiar strategies at work in this essay.

Developing the Reflections. This section helps students to understand that a successful reflective essay is generally a balance of general ideas or statements on the one hand, and specific examples on the other, and that the relationship between the general and the specific in a reflective essay is likely to be highly symbiotic, as each strategy is used successfully mainly in relation to the other. This activity asks students to identify and analyze both general and specific material in Toussaint's essay, directing them toward specific paragraphs as they analyze and write.

Maintaining Topical Coherence. One of the greatest challenges facing writers of reflective essays, as students are bound to discover as they begin their own drafts, is to maintain a sense of coherence, a controlling idea which underlies and makes relevant seemingly disparate material. As students analyze and write about whether and how Toussaint sustains this coherence, we direct their attention toward her use of cues for the reader, including transitions between paragraphs and repetition of thematic material.

Engaging Readers. This section helps students see that, particularly in reflective writing, personal engagement on the part of the writer invites the same on the part of the reader. However, as they reread and analyze Toussaint's essay, students are encouraged to consider not only the personal but the social significance of her reflections. As part of the point of the reflective essay is its commentary on larger human experience, this will be an important consideration for students beginning their own reflective writing.

RESOURCES FOR TEACHING THE READINGS

This chapter offers six readings of varying length and difficulty, including the sample essay by Nicollette Toussaint described in the preceding section. The next essay, by Brent Staples, takes on another serious subject: our cultural attitudes toward gender and racial difference. Barbara Ehrenreich reflects on the disturbing issue of family violence. Ishmael Reed's essay is a meditation on multiculturalism. Diana Trilling's essay once again picks up the theme of gender difference, while the final essay, by student Katherine Haines, continues this theme, this time in the context of self-perception.

The following material introduces each reading and explores the possibilities for classroom use of the sections on reading for meaning and reading like a writer and the ideas for writing that follow each essay.

Brent Staples, **Black Men and Public Space**

The introductory note to this essay reminds students that reflective essays are based on a combination of particular occasion and general reflection; you might also encourage students very directly to read it in the context of what they have learned from their examination of the sample essay by Nicollette Toussaint.

Reading for Meaning

This section directs students back to the text to explore their own understanding of and response to Staples's essay. Students are also invited to read Staples's essay in light of their own experience, and to identify with Staples himself as well as his "victim."

Extending Meaning through Conversation. In this activity, students are encouraged to develop their understanding of the meaning of Staples's essay by discussing it with one or two other students. As this piece touches on issues of race and gender, you may find that students have particularly strong feelings about it; once students have explored the meaning of the essay in small groups, you might facilitate a class discussion revolving around these issues. Another option would be to ask each pair or group to report briefly in class on any notable differences that remain after discussion; you might then lead a class discussion about the acceptability—and even usefulness—of such differences among readers.

Looking for Patterns of Opposition (A Further Strategy for Reading for Meaning). This task calls students' attention to the oppositions within the essay, perhaps beginning with the discrepancies between how Staples views himself and how others view him. Students are referred to Appendix 1, A Catalog of Critical Reading Strategies. Expect students to need some guidance in getting started with this exercise, as well as in exploring the implications of these oppositions.

As usual following the first reading in each chapter, you might want to collect students' writing based on these activities, partly in order to monitor how well they are grasping the material and partly so that you can share aloud a sample of student responses.

Reading like a Writer: Presenting the Particular Occasion

This section calls attention to the particular occasion out of which Staples's reflection develops. Students who have completed the autobiographical assignment in Chapter 2 should be prepared to analyze the building of tension in this brief narrative; if you have not yet discussed narrative with your students, this question offers a good opportunity to do so. Whether or not your students have worked with Chapter 2, we once again suggest that you lead your class as a group in the analysis portion of this activity for the first reading of the chapter, showing them explicitly how to annotate and take useful notes on the reading. Students should be able to note the specificity of Staples's nouns and verbs—the economical but vivid narration of the specific action of the "characters" in the occasion. We also draw students' attention to the relationship between the particular occasion and the more general subject of Staples's reflection.

Compare. It is important at this stage that students recognize the variety of particular occasions open to them as prospective writers of reflective essays. This activity, whether students complete it individually or in groups, should also help them focus on how occasions are used by different writers.

Considering Ideas for Your Own Writing

Staples's essay calls attention to the way Americans, as a society, conceive of public and private space. To write on this subject, students would have to do some observational or field research. You might suggest that they study spatial relationships among people in different places and situations—a shopping mall, a football game, a large party, waiting for a movie, on a bus or train. They also might look at spatial relationships among different groups—men and women, the elderly and the young, people at work and people at play.

Barbara Ehrenreich, **Are Families Dangerous?**

Students may find this essay, like several of the selections in the chapter, not merely thought provoking, but disturbing. These readings should help students see that, while the purpose of reflective writing is not to take a stand or to exhort its readers to action, it can nonetheless evoke powerful responses in its readers.

Reading for Meaning

In this section, students are asked to consider Ehrenreich's purpose and audience, beginning by considering the precise nature of the dangers she locates within the family. Students are also invited to recall their own experiences in the context of Ehrenreich's reflections. Because this essay may elicit highly personal responses from some students, you may find that you need to help students stay focused on the essay itself, making explicit connections between their experiences and the text.

Extending Meaning through Conversation. Here, we encourage students to enhance their understanding of Ehrenreich's essay by discussing it with one or two other students. While many students will recognize, either intuitively or from experience, the dangers Ehrenreich identifies, others may be put off by what they perceive to be an attack on "family values." As students explore these tensions in conversation, they also gain a fuller understanding of Ehrenreich's reflections.

Reading like a Writer: Maintaining Topical Coherence

Students should recall from their work with the sample essay in this chapter that although reflective essays tend to appear casual on the surface, their writers actually work hard to maintain topical coherence. Here, we draw students' attention to the cues Ehrenreich uses to help readers follow her reflections, including transitions, topic sentences, and repeated words and phrases. If students have a hard time getting started on this activity, you could point out the repetition in the first few paragraphs of "nest" and "cradle" (paragraph 2) and "lie down" (paragraphs 3 and 5) as a possible starting point.

Considering Ideas for Your Own Writing

Like the preceding essays in this chapter focusing on racism and disability, Ehrenreich's selection deals with a difficult topic. Here, we ask students to consider taking on a similar challenge, writing their own reflective essays about subjects that are not often openly discussed. Especially if students are basing their essays on personal experience, you may find that emotional distance becomes an issue; if your students have already worked with Chapter 2: Autobiography, you might refer them back to pertinent sections of that chapter.

Ishmael Reed, **What's American about America?**

This essay takes up the fascinating and timely concept of multiculturalism. In the headnote, students are encouraged to consider what they already know about this subject.

Reading for Meaning
Here, students are asked to respond in some depth to Reed's reflections on the cultural diversity of American society. As with many of the readings in this text, students are invited to relate Reed's reflections to their own observations and experiences. Depending on the demographics of your particular student population, this exercise is likely to elicit a rich range of interesting responses. If students do rely on their personal experiences to make meaning from the selection, you will want to be sure that they do not move too far from the essay itself; one way of making sure you can encourage them to make explicit connections between the text and their own experience is to invite them to share their responses orally in class.

Extending Meaning through Conversation. Once again, students are invited to explore the meaning of a reading by discussing it with one or two other students. Because students are likely to have strong personal responses to this particular essay, you might find it useful to circulate among pairs or groups, making sure students are making connections between their experience and Reed's essay.

Reading like a Writer: Developing the Reflections by Piling Up Examples
Students will notice immediately that, unlike the other selections in the chapter, Reed's essay opens with a series of occasions. Most students will note that the diversity of this series is appropriate to the subject on which Reed proceeds to reflect. Students are also asked to scrutinize Reed's use of examples throughout the essay, and to comment in detail on their function in Reed's reflections. Careful readers will see that some of Reed's examples, such as that of the Puritans (paragraphs 10–12) support a distinctly critical perspective; as with the preceding selection by Barbara Ehrenreich, students may be divided as to whether or not this is appropriate in reflective writing. In order to facilitate fruitful discussion here, you might ask a few students to read their responses aloud to the class.

Considering Ideas for Your Own Writing
This section invites students to consider their own experiences with or observations of cultural diversity as a basis for their reflective writing. Again, this is likely to be a valuable source of possible topics for many of your students.

Diana Trilling, **On Sexual Separatism**

The introductory material to this piece highlights the main ideas of Trilling's essay, and notes that students may find these ideas somewhat surprising. As with other selections in this chapter, we aim to help students see that reflective essays may take on difficult and even disturbing topics, and may do so in ways that may challenge readers to question their own assumptions.

Reading for Meaning

Students are encouraged to reread the text closely, beginning by speculating about Trilling's purpose in writing this essay. We provide some further suggestions to help students develop their understanding of the meaning of the piece.

Extending Meaning through Conversation. Here we invite students to enhance their understanding by discussing the essay with one or two other students. Trilling's reflections are likely to elicit lively discussion; you might allow some time in class for students to share their ideas once they have explored them in small groups. You may find that, as in the case of Ehrenreich's essay, the responses of male and female students differ here.

Reading like a Writer: Developing the Reflections through Comparison and Contrast

Strategies of comparison and contrast may be familiar to students from their high school experiences with writing; this section should help them to see how useful these strategies can be to writers of reflective essays. We ask students to examine Trilling's use of comparison and contrast closely, and to write briefly about her use of these strategies.

Considering Ideas for Your Own Writing

Students are invited to consider writing their own reflective essays on either same- or opposite-gender relations, beginning by identifying a specific occasion which might elicit such reflections.

Katherine Haines, **Whose Body Is This?**

Like the essays by Brent Staples, Barbara Ehrenreich, and Diana Trilling, this essay reflects, in part, on gender distinctions and self-concepts. Although the topic may be serious, most students will find this essay accessible and easy to read.

Reading for Meaning

Because Haines is so open about her own feelings and experiences (and perhaps because, unlike the other writers represented in this chapter, she is a fellow student and not a professional author), students are likely to have a fairly distinct impression of Haines as a person. When it comes to identifying their own experiences and observations with Haines's, though, you may once again see a certain discrepancy between the responses of male and female students.

Extending Meaning through Conversation. We try to encourage students to acknowledge and comment on this discrepancy in this activity, in which they will discuss their understanding of the meaning of the essay with one or two other students. As always, if you find students are relying perhaps too heavily on personal experience in interpreting the reading, you could check this tendency by moving among pairs or groups, helping students make explicit connections between their experiences and the text.

Reading like a Writer: Engaging Readers

This section helps students to see the ways in which writers of reflective essays are aware of their readers. We ask students to reread, analyze, and write briefly about Haines's attention to her audience, focusing on the techniques she uses to engage and sustain the interest of her readers. Students are likely to differ somewhat on how successful Haines is at engaging her readers' interest; asking a few students to share their responses to this activity in class may elicit a useful discussion of this important aspect of the genre.

<u>Compare</u>. As they embark on their own reflective essays, students will find it useful to compare the variety of ways, ranging from cajoling to challenging in tone, in which different writers attempt to engage their readers.

Reading like a Writer: A Follow-up Activity

As students complete the Reading like a Writer activities throughout the chapter, they will generate a substantial amount of writing on the reading selections. In order to enhance further their understanding of the genre, you might ask students to review their writing, selecting one piece to revise and extend by doing more analysis. This expanded piece of writing would be turned in along with the essay package or in students' end-of-course portfolios.

Considering Ideas for Your Own Writing

Issues related to cultural ideals of "beauty" and "success" tend to lurk just below the surface of most of our students' awareness, providing a rich source of topic possibilities for reflective essays. You might encourage students to consider this type of subject from different perspectives; while students may naturally approach these issues on a very personal basis, they can also examine them on broader cultural and historical levels.

THINKING ABOUT WHAT MAKES REFLECTIVE WRITING EFFECTIVE

Once again, we give students a chance to review and consolidate what they have learned by reading a number of writing selections in a particular genre. Referring students back to the Guide to Reading Reflective Writing following the sample essay by Nicollette Toussaint at the beginning of the chapter, we ask students to select an essay they feel to be especially effective in fulfilling the basic features of successful reflective writing, and to write briefly about their reasons for selecting this piece. Whether students complete this activity individually or in small groups, you might plan some time in class for them to share their responses.

A GUIDE TO REFLECTIVE WRITING

The guide leads students through a composing process that follows these stages:

Invention
    Finding a Particular Occasion and General Subject
    Choosing a Subject
    Developing the Particular Occasion
        Learning More about Your Readers: A Collaborative Activity
    Developing Your Reflections on the Subject
        Generalize about It
        Give Examples of It
        Compare and Contrast It
        Extend It
        Analyze It
        Apply It

As they search for topics for their own essays, encourage students to think in terms of both general subjects and particular occasions. The most important point is that there must be corresponding entries in the two columns of their invention chart. For every general subject there must be at least one particular example to illustrate it; for each particular occasion students must think of at least one general idea it embodies. This correspondence between the abstract and the particular is the most crucial element in reflective writing.

Notice the final comment on the topic chart in the text. Students may complete much of it at one sitting, but they should spread their topic selection process over several days, returning to review and add to their charts every day. This will allow them to reconsider their ideas and discover others they did not think of earlier.

After students have made a tentative selection, the exploratory writing exercise labeled Choosing a Subject is a valuable investment of time. If the topic proves promising, they can use the ideas they have written; if the exercise reveals that they have less to say than they had thought, the fifteen minutes spent exploring the topic will have saved them from wasting even more time trying to write a draft on that topic.

Students accustomed to writing only for teachers may not immediately see the purpose of analyzing their readers. If they found some of the selections in this chapter easier to read and understand than the others, you might refer to this experience to demonstrate that writers make different assumptions about their readers and modify their writing accordingly. The guide offers further advice on writing for particular readers in the Setting Goals section.

SPECIAL PROBLEMS OF THIS WRITING ASSIGNMENT. In our experience, problems student writers have with this assignment fall into two fairly predictable categories: choosing workable subjects (see Promising and Unpromising Topics below) and developing their reflections on these subjects. In the latter area, students' difficulties mainly have to do with achieving some balance between particular material—in the form of occasions, examples, and illustrations—and general statements. Exploratory drafts tend toward one extreme or the other. As our students begin writing, we often see first drafts that either look very much like essays about events (especially if students have recently completed the autobiographical assignment in Chapter 2) based completely on particular occasions, or that consist almost entirely of vague, abstract statements. A third type of problem draft comes to us from students who believe they need to reach some kind of conclusion about their subject, perhaps anticipating upcoming argument assignments. All of these types of problems can be minimized if you help students pay careful attention to both the general and the particular components of each reading selection as well as of their own developing essays.

PROMISING AND UNPROMISING TOPICS. Although students will have had quite a bit of practice selecting and working with various topic possibilities during the collaborative activity early in the chapter and as they read the Considering Ideas for Your Own Writing sections following each reading, you may be surprised at how much difficulty they encounter in actually settling on subjects for their own essays. Once again, these problems are generally reflected in three distinct ways: on the one hand is the student who confuses the subject of the essay with the particular occasion that triggers the reflection; on the other hand is the student who takes on a very abstract concept (love, truth, justice, etc.) and then is paralyzed by his or her inability to ground the subject in concrete occasions, examples, and illustrations. A third type of student will want to "reflect" on a controversial issue such as abortion or capital punishment, and is very likely to wind up writing a position paper rather than a reflective essay. As instructors, it is easy for us to see that each of these types of topics might in fact be perfectly appropriate for a reflective essay; our task is to help students see that their problems may not be with topic choice itself, but with how they plan to handle these topics in the context of the reflection essay. You may find that you need to coach students individually through these early stages of the writing process.

Chapter 5 EXPLAINING CONCEPTS

If your students are going from Chapter 4: Reflection, to Chapter 5, you might take time to discuss the similarities and differences between reflective and explanatory writing. Like reflective writing, writing to explain a concept often begins with particular firsthand observations and then "moves beyond description of specific objects and scenes to general concepts and ideas," as the introductory note to the chapter indicates. However, whereas the purpose of reflective writing is to try out the writer's ideas and help the reader see even the familiar in a new light, the main purpose of explanatory writing is just that—to explain something to the reader. While explanatory writing may be every bit as entertaining and thought-provoking as a reflective essay, it never loses sight of its primary goal: to inform the reader.

Likewise, if your students are going directly from Chapter 3 to Chapter 5, you might want to point out some of the similarities and differences between observational and explanatory writing. Both aim to present information in a way that readers will find intelligible and interesting. Observational writing derives mainly from the writer's firsthand experiences and observation, and it often relies on narrative and vivid description to communicate what the writer has seen or learned about the subject. Explanatory writing, on the other hand, typically derives from a variety of sources that may include the writer's personal experience and observation but usually depends heavily on what the writer has learned from others through reading and listening. Writers of explanation synthesize, review, or summarize the work of others. They present information, draw connections, and discuss implications. They may also translate technical or specialized information to the language and contexts of readers outside the discipline.

In this chapter, we focus on a particular aim of explanatory writing—writing to explain concepts. This focus enables students to work on the kind of explanation they are reading and writing in most of their courses. Throughout the disciplines, particularly in introductory courses, students are learning basic concepts. They learn by reading and by writing. Understanding the rhetoric of explanatory discourse can help them become better learners as well as more effective explainers.

WRITING ASSIGNMENT: Explaining Concepts

This is the writing assignment that appears near the beginning of Chapter 5:

> Write an essay that explains a concept. Choose a concept that interests you and that you want to study further. Consider carefully what your readers already know about the concept and how your essay might add to what they know.

Possible essay topics (Considering Ideas for Your Own Writing) follow each reading, and additional suggested concepts appear in the Invention section of the Guide to Writing Explanations of Concepts.

Writing Situations for Explaining Concepts

The writing situations that open this chapter demonstrate a wide range of academic and non-academic occasions for explaining concepts and educating readers about a subject. The situations involve a wide variety of sources of information, as well as a variety of writing strategies. Students can readily see why readers will need or want to know the information explained by each writer. They can also see how these writers purposefully seek to increase their readers' knowledge of and appreciation for a concept.

Practicing Explaining Concepts: A Collaborative Activity

This activity gives students their first classroom opportunity to explain a concept, in this case orally, briefly, and informally, to a small group of their peers. This activity should not take more than twenty minutes or so. The list of possible concepts is diverse enough to allow sufficient choice. Before they begin the activity, you could review with students the interactive nature of the exercise: following each mini-presentation, listeners share with the presenter something they learned about the concept. Part 2 requires students to distance themselves from explaining concepts in order to reflect on what they have learned about the genre. You may have to encourage them to move to part 2. Whole-class follow-up can refocus on the questions at the end of the activity; this discussion should be productive as students will already have examined these questions in their small groups.

A GUIDE TO READING ESSAYS EXPLAINING CONCEPTS

This section once again guides students through the reading of an essay on two levels: as readers and as prospective writers of explanatory pieces. For class activities to use in conjunction with this section, see Part 5 of this manual.

After a brief illustration of annotation, we provide students with a sample essay by David Quammen. Most students will find this essay to be thoroughly entertaining and informative. It shows that explanatory writing need not be dry or dull, and that scientific concepts can be truly fascinating. Although he is not a scientist, Quammen comes across as an expert on the subject: his expertise, like that of most students themselves, comes from research into secondary sources.

Reading for Meaning

From the headnote to the selection, students know that Quammen's readers are interested in, but not necessarily highly informed about, topics relating to nature and the environment. Here we invite students to comment briefly on what Quammen's essay has taught them about parthenogenesis; we then provide a number of suggestions to help them develop their responses. If time permits, you might give students a few minutes of class time to discuss their responses, either in small groups or as a class. Perhaps especially if you have students from a variety of academic backgrounds, discussion will help students to consider the writer's awareness of his readers and how much they are likely to know about his topic.

Reading like a Writer

In this section, we help students shift their focus from the content and purpose of the essay to the strategies the writer uses in achieving that purpose. These strategies include *devising a readable plan, using appropriate explanatory strategies, using sources responsibly,* and *engaging readers' interest.* In the critical reading and writing tasks that follow, each general strategy is broken down more specifically: *devising a readable plan* calls students' attention to the cueing strategies Quammen and other writers use to make their essays "reader-friendly," while *using appropriate explanatory strategies* offers students a brief catalog of the types of rhetorical strategies writers in this genre find most useful. The section called *using sources responsibly* helps students to understand that writers must select sources purposefully and integrate them smoothly into the explanation. Finally, *engaging readers' interest* invites students to consider the strategies writers of potentially dry explanations of abstract concepts use to attract and sustain reader interest. In each of these sections, we ask students to analyze Quammen's use of the strategy in question, and then to write briefly based on their analyses.

The Reading like a Writer section following the sample essay offers a comprehensive catalog of these strategies. Corresponding sections following each of the subsequent readings in the chapter focus closely on individual strategies; in each case, students are asked to analyze the writer's use of a particular strategy and to report the results of their analyses.

Devising a Readable Plan. This section encourages students to examine the organization of Quammen's essay, focusing in particular on the cueing devices he and other successful writers use in explaining concepts which are likely to be unfamiliar to their readers. To illustrate these cueing devices, we call attention to Quammen's use of a forecasting statement,

73

topic sentences, transitions, and summaries; students will want to keep these in mind as they begin to plan their own essays. While these devices will be familiar to many of your students, you might find it useful to walk the class through part or all of Quammen's essay, making sure students can identify where and how Quammen uses each. In addition to focusing on transitions between paragraphs, students should be able to identify readily Quammen's brief use of forecasting (in paragraph 2, for instance) and summary.

Using Appropriate Writing Strategies. This exercise will be central in its importance to students both as readers and as writers of essays explaining concepts; the strategies discussed here will also figure prominently in upcoming chapters in this textbook. While this section introduces students to six specific strategies, it asks them to focus on any one in particular; thus, you can expect a range of responses to this task. Once again, although your students may be familiar with these strategies (many, for instance, will have written "comparison and contrast" essays in high school), they may need extra help in identifying precisely how each functions in Quammen's essay; the text provides paragraph references to help them get started. You might ask students who have focused on different strategies to share their written responses to this exercise briefly in class.

Using Sources Responsibly. One important decision students will need to make as they write their own essays is which source material to summarize, which to paraphrase and which to quote directly. This task asks students to consider Quammen's decision in paragraphs 11 and 16 to quote directly, and to note the smooth integration of the quotations into his own text. This exercise is particularly important, as many students fail to realize how vital the responsible use of sources will be to their success in writing at the college level.

Engaging Readers' Interest. Most students are likely to note that the first paragraph engages readers' curiosity even before Quammen names and defines the concept in the penultimate sentence. Paragraph 4, like paragraph 2, uses direct address to get readers' attention. Paragraphs 10 and 12 present the presumed advantages of parthenogenesis—both aphids and humans—in a witty way, which most students will appreciate but which some may find heavy-handed.

If your students have completed the assignment presented in Chapter 3: Observation, they will be quite familiar with the goal of at once entertaining and informing readers, and with the challenge of meting out potentially dry information carefully so that it does not lessen the more entertaining aspect of the essay. Students should be able to report in some detail on Quammen's handling of these challenges.

RESOURCES FOR TEACHING THE READINGS

This chapter has five readings, including the sample essay by David Quammen described in the preceding section. All of the selections explain a concept in a particular discipline or field. Perry Nodelman discusses "reading against texts," a concept from contemporary literary theory, while Deborah Tannen introduces a concept from linguistics: "markedness." Philip Elmer-DeWitt explains the concept of cyberspace; Mihaly Csikszentmilhalyi presents the

74

psychological concept of the autotelic self. Our last selection is written by student Melissa McCool, who explains the concept of reincarnation.

The following material discusses each reading and offers advice on using the sections on reading for meaning and reading like a writer and the ideas for writing that follow each selection.

Perry Nodelman, **Reading against Texts**

As is the case with many essays explaining concepts, the concept introduced by Perry Nodelman calls into question previously held assumptions, in this case about the reading process.

Reading for Meaning

This section helps students extend and clarify their understanding of Nodelman's essay by explaining in their own words the concept of reading against the text, as well as the rather abstract subconcepts Nodelman uses in his own explanation. As usual, this section also invites students to explore their understanding of the concept by applying it to their own experience. If students do use their personal experience to make meaning from the text, you might invite them to do so orally in class; in this way, you can be sure that students who do use personal experience aren't moving too far away from the text itself, but that they return to the essay to make the connections between their experiences and the text explicit. Also, as usual with the first reading selection in each chapter, you might consider collecting students' writing for this activity, looking over it quickly, and reading some responses out loud to your class. This not only helps you monitor how well students are understanding the reading, but also allows you to provide examples of more or less successful responses to the activity.

Extending Meaning through Conversation. This activity, which follows each of the readings in the textbook, invites students to develop their understanding of each text more fully by discussing it with one or two other students. Especially after the first reading in each chapter, you might set aside some class time to discuss with the class as a group how the activity went and what meanings seemed to emerge from conversations.

Questioning to Understand and Remember (A Further Strategy for Reading for Meaning). Here, we refer students to Appendix 1, A Catalog of Critical Reading Strategies, where they will find this strategy demonstrated on a sample text. Students may be surprised at how useful this fairly simple strategy can be in helping them identify, understand, and remember the main points of difficult texts. You might point out that, in addition to helping students understand Nodelman's essay, this strategy will stand them in good stead throughout their academic careers.

By completing at least the first set of Reading for Meaning activities—those following the first reading in each chapter—together in class, with you leading and taking notes on the board, you can help students understand how these activities work, and remind them of the need to continue to reread and annotate each selection.

Reading like a Writer: Devising a Readable Plan

Students are likely to have noticed Nodelman's use of headings to indicate the division of information; here, we call their attention to his use of forecasting and of topic sentences as well. These strategies should be familiar to students from their reading of the essay by David

Quammen earlier in the chapter, but analyzing and writing briefly about Nodelman's use of these cueing devices will help students further appreciate their importance in this type of writing. As usual with the first reading in each chapter, you might lead students through the analysis section, showing them how to do a thorough analysis by annotating and taking notes. Once students have completed both the analysis and writing portions of this activity, you might either collect their responses and skim them briefly or have students share them orally in class, keeping a list on the board in either case of the cueing devices students locate in the essay.

Considering Ideas for Your Own Writing

This section steers students toward literary studies or composition theory and rhetoric as a possible source of topics for their own essays. Encourage students not only to choose a potential topic, but to consider the specific writing strategies they might use in explaining the concept they've chosen.

Deborah Tannen, Marked Women

Some of your students may already be familiar with Tannen's work through her best-selling books; nearly all students will find her essay on linguistic markedness and its implications for gender relations interesting and provocative.

Reading for Meaning

As usual, this section directs students back to the text, asking them to explore and clarify their understanding of the essay by paraphrasing Tannen's explanation of the concept of linguistic markedness. We give students several suggestions for developing their understanding of the concept; you may find that they are also interested in relating it to their own experiences as either men or women. Because students are likely to find Tannen's topic particularly provocative, you may find that you need to monitor their responses, either by collecting and skimming their writing or by having them share their thoughts in class, in order to make sure they are not straying too far from the text itself as they bring to bear their personal experiences.

Extending Meaning through Conversation. As we do following each reading selection, we encourage students here to explore the meaning of the essay in more detail by talking about it with one or two other students. Once again, because this particular essay raises some sensitive issues, you may find that you need to help students keep on track, perhaps by circulating among pairs or groups of students.

Reading like a Writer: Explaining through Illustration

This section calls students' attention to the importance of the use of concrete illustration in explaining abstract concepts. While students should be able to readily identify Tannen's use of illustration throughout the essay, we ask them to scrutinize two sections in particular, looking for ways in which the illustrations Tannen chooses allow her to draw larger generalizations about her topic. We also ask students to comment on whether they feel Tannen's explicit connection between the illustrations and the concept of markedness is helpful to them as readers. Some students are likely to find Tannen's interpretations somewhat off-putting; you might help students to speculate about what other options Tannen might have had in explaining her subject.

76

Considering Ideas for Your Own Writing
The fields of linguistics, gender studies, and sociology offer a wealth of topics for this essay. You might want to remind students that they needn't already be experts in any of these areas in order to write successful explanations of concepts, and that, in fact, writing on a topic about which they are just learning themselves may offer certain advantages, as students may be more likely to anticipate what their audience does or does not already know about the concept.

Philip Elmer-DeWitt, **Welcome to Cyberspace**

Students should find Elmer-DeWitt's essay interesting and accessible. Like David Quammen in his essay explaining the concept of parthenogenesis, which appears as the sample essay earlier in the chapter, Elmer-DeWitt presents potentially complex scientific information in—for the most part—layperson's terms.

Reading for Meaning
Where students were asked to explore their understanding of the previous essay by paraphrasing its main concept, here, we ask students to develop their understanding of the essay by summarizing. You may find this a useful opportunity to review for students the difference between these two reading (and writing) strategies, as well as to foreground once again the value of rereading and annotating. We also provide a number of other suggestions for further exploring the meaning of the essay as students write briefly about it.

Extending Meaning through Conversation. In this section, we once again invite students to explore their understanding of the piece in more depth by discussing it with other students. While Elmer-DeWitt's essay is perhaps less likely than the previous selection to raise sensitive social issues, students should still have much to say on the timely subject of cyberspace.

Reading like a Writer: Explaining through Comparison and Contrast
This section once again refers students to the list of writing strategies following the sample essay by David Quammen. Many students will find the use of comparison and contrast a valuable strategy as they embark on their own explanations of concepts; encourage them to complete this activity thoroughly and thoughtfully.

Compare. This activity, which follows one or two readings in each chapter, helps students focus on how different writers make use of the same set of strategies—in this case, comparison and contrast. We draw students' attention to two other readings in the chapter. You might want to encourage students to comment on why, where both Tannen and Csikszentmilhalyi rely primarily on contrast in explaining their topics, Elmer-DeWitt finds comparison a more useful strategy, as it helps his readers relate the abstract concept of cyberspace to their everyday experience with such objects as telephones.

Considering Ideas for Your Own Writing
You and your students may have already discovered, through previous activities following this reading selection, that students are likely to bring a wide variety of computer experience into the classroom. Once again, you might point out that, while the topics suggested here may seem ideal for computer science majors, students need not be experts in a particular

field to write a successful essay explaining a topic. We also invite students to consider using strategies of comparison or contrast in explaining this type of topic.

Mihaly Csikszentmilhalyi, **The Autotelic Self**

Where previous selections in this chapter have explained concepts from linguistics, sociology, and the sciences, this selection deals with a concept from the field of psychology. As they read, students may find it useful to keep in mind that, like Tannen and (to some extent) Nodelman, Csikszentmilhalyi is a specialist writing for non-specialists, whereas Quammen, for instance, writes as a nonscientist about a scientific topic. Students might want to consider how this difference affects each writer's choice of strategies.

Reading for Meaning
As always in this section, students are asked to explore their understanding of the selection by responding to the content of the text; we give them a number of fairly specific suggestions for writing briefly about the selection. If your students have worked with Chapter 2: Autobiography in this text, they may find it particularly interesting to apply the author's concept of the autotelic self to one (or more) of the essays in that chapter.

Extending Meaning through Conversation. Especially in the case of a complex and unfamiliar topic such as the one dealt with in this essay, students are likely to find it useful to explore their understanding of the essay further by discussing it with one or two other students. Because students may have trouble getting started on this activity, we draw their attention to possible starting points; you might also allow them to relate the concept to their own experiences, as long as this does not lead them too far from the text itself.

Summarizing (A Further Strategy for Reading for Meaning). Students will already be familiar with summarizing from their work earlier in the chapter. Here, referring students to Appendix 1, A Catalog of Critical Reading Strategies, we give students the opportunity to practice the strategy, a critical reading technique they will find useful throughout their reading for this and other courses, in more detail. You might collect and quickly skim students' responses to this task to make sure they are on the right track.

Reading like a Writer: Explaining through Narrating a Process
In this section, as we do following each reading, we ask students to analyze and write briefly about a specific strategy used by the writer. If your students have worked with Chapter 2: Autobiography, they will already be familiar with narrative as a writing strategy; here, we aim to show them that this strategy can be as useful for writers of explanation as it is for autobiographers. You might introduce this activity by discussing in class the differences students are likely to see between the use of narrative in the two chapters. If your students have not read Chapter 2, you can still help them see that concepts often involve processes, and to pinpoint how two writers from the present chapter use narrative to describe these processes.

Considering Ideas for Your Own Writing
This section asks students to imagine writing about a concept from the field of psychology. Students are directed to basic references in their college libraries to get ideas for possible topics; as students will almost certainly be using the library regardless of the topics they ultimately choose, this activity is a good way of introducing them to reference sources.

Students are also invited to begin thinking about the specific writing strategies they will use in writing their own essays.

Melissa McCool, **Reincarnation**

As they read this essay by student Melissa McCool, students will notice her extensive and careful use of source material. You might encourage students to keep track of the proportion of the essay McCool devotes to sources in relation to her own commentary and analysis.

Reading for Meaning

As always, this section directs students back to the text of the essay, asking them to further their understanding of the concept of reincarnation by briefly summarizing McCool's explanation. In addition to once again highlighting the importance of rereading and annotating, this section invites students to develop their understanding of the concept by putting it in the context of their own prior knowledge and/or religious or spiritual beliefs.

Extending Meaning through Conversation. As students discuss their understanding of McCool's explanation of reincarnation in pairs or small groups, they will find that they gain a better sense of the meaning of the essay; we give them a number of suggestions for getting their discussions started. Especially if your students come from a variety of religious backgrounds and/or feel strongly about religious beliefs, you might find it useful to move from group to group, getting an idea how discussions are going and helping them stay focused on the meaning of McCool's essay.

Reading like a Writer: Using Sources

The careful use of sources is likely to be crucial to the success of each student's essay explaining a concept. This section helps students focus closely on McCool's use of sources. While some students may feel that McCool relies too heavily on published sources, they should be able to report that the source material she uses is generally integrated smoothly into her own text, and that her sources are carefully documented. Once again, you might remind students how important the skillful use of sources will be as they write at the college level.

Reading like a Writer: A Follow-up Activity

Once students have completed all of the Reading like a Writer activities in the chapter, they will have accumulated a substantial amount of written commentary about the reading selections. Don't overlook the usefulness of having them review their writings, selecting one to revise and extend by doing further analysis. Students would turn this expanded piece in with their essay packages, or include it in their end-of-course portfolios.

Considering Ideas for Your Own Writing

Religion and philosophy provide a wealth of topic possibilities for student writers. Students with strong religious beliefs, however, may need to be reminded that the purpose of this type of essay is *explanatory*, not persuasive or judgmental. We invite students to begin thinking not only about possible topics for their own essays, but also about their own use of sources.

THINKING ABOUT WHAT MAKES ESSAYS EXPLAINING CONCEPTS EFFECTIVE

As we do following the readings in each chapter, we ask students here to review and consolidate what they have learned about writing in a genre. Referring students back to the list of features—originally presented following the sample essay in the chapter introduction—of successful essays of this type, we invite students to choose the one essay from the chapter they feel to be most successful in achieving its purpose and fulfilling these features. Asking students to justify their choices helps them focus even more closely on the features of the genre.

A GUIDE TO WRITING ESSAYS EXPLAINING CONCEPTS

The guide leads students through the following steps:

Invention
    Listing Possible Concepts
    Choosing a Concept
    Analyzing Your Readers
    Finding Out More about Your Concept
        Finding Information at the Library or on the Internet
        Consulting an Expert
        Focusing Your Research
        An Example: Melissa McCool's Research Process
    Deciding Which Explanatory Strategies to Use
    Beginning
        Learning More about Your Readers: A Collaborative Activity
Drafting
    Setting Goals
    Planning Your Draft
Reading a Draft Critically
    Reading for a First Impression
    Reading to Analyze
        Using Appropriate Explanatory Strategies
        Making the Draft Readable
        Using Sources Responsibly
        Engaging Readers
Revising
    Revising to Improve the Plan
    Revising the Explanatory Strategies
    Revising the Use of Sources
    Revising to Engage Readers
Reflecting on What You Have Learned about Writing Concept Explanations

A number of points in this composing process need special emphasis. The first is topic choice. Students may not already be experts on their topics, but their writing improves when they have a genuine curiosity about the subject. If a student neither knows nor cares much about a topic, good writing is unlikely to result.

When they first choose topics, students often think in broad terms, so you may need to help them narrow their topics to the point where they can produce explanatory essays of suitable depth.

The biggest challenge for writers of explanatory discourse is selecting and arranging the material in a way that will be clear and interesting to readers. Three steps in the composing process address this problem, and students should give them special attention: analyzing readers' knowledge, needs, and interest in the subject; deciding which explanatory strategies to use; and working out an organizational plan for the essay. Thinking carefully about these three steps—and then following through with a rich, exploratory period of invention writing—can help prevent students' essays from being dry, dull lists of information.

SPECIAL PROBLEMS OF THIS WRITING ASSIGNMENT. In our experience, the main problems that student writers have in this assignment fall into two categories: choosing an appropriate concept and then analyzing and synthesizing the available information on it. One solution to the problem of topic choice is to encourage students to write about subjects introduced in their other courses. In the invention section, some academic subjects are suggested. This assignment lends itself to cross-disciplinary writing.

If students lack confidence in writing about academic subjects, you might allow them to write about concepts drawn from extracurricular interests.

Students may ask you "What *is* a concept?" We propose an answer that paraphrases the dictionary definition: "a general idea derived from specific instances." Each reading in this chapter enables students to understand that many specific observations or instances lead to a concept and eventually to its particular name. It is interesting to consider that certain concepts can be intuited or fully recognized long before they are named.

Students will need your help in finding a focus for their essays. Many concepts are too big—too much is known about them—for a college essay, even one of substantial length. Consequently, you will likely want them to write about one *aspect* of the concept. Notice how the invention activities are set up to lead students first to a broad overview of the concept and then to a focus on one interesting aspect of it. Only with a focus in mind do they begin collecting research information.

For this assignment we approve both the concept-choice and the concept-focus. At both stages, we hear from each student and involve the whole class in evaluating topic choices and foci.

Presenting a technical concept in a way that is clear and interesting to a general audience challenges student writers. Students may become very concerned with the specificity and accuracy of the information they report, and, in the process, forget about engaging readers' interest. The purpose of the essay is to give readers interesting new knowledge. The greatest challenge of this assignment may not be the gathering and reporting of information, but the presenting of information in a way that allows readers to understand key terms, follow the organization of the essay, and remain interested in the topic. To succeed with this challenge, students will need to pay particular attention to the tone they use, the cues they provide for readers, and the defining and classifying strategies they use.

The assignment can also be a good way to introduce students to library research. The student who knows little about a concept but is curious about it can gather information from the library or by talking with experts. You may want to require some library research from all students. Both firsthand and secondary research strategies are covered in some detail in Appendix 2; you might want to refer students to this section of the text fairly early in the assignment.

Still another problem with this writing task is that student writers may allow themselves to be eclipsed by their sources. Their essays then become dumping grounds for unprocessed information, leaving readers to guess at its significance. Remind students that they must use sources judiciously, providing enough of their own commentary to help readers interpret the significance of source material. Referring students back to the reading selections in the chapter will help them to see how other writers have handled this challenge.

A related challenge is the problem of selecting and arranging the information, using the range of available strategies to achieve the purpose. Student writers often have difficulty designing a plan that will organize the information in a way readers will find interesting and comprehensible. A common problem is the essay that grasps at a simple, ready-made structure, often following the writer's process of discovering the information and ignoring what readers know or need to know about the subject. Again, analyzing the structure of the readings can show students how to avoid this problem.

PROMISING AND UNPROMISING TOPICS. The least problematic topics are those which are inherently concepts, such as existentialism or bilingualism. Students who choose such topics will probably have little difficulty finding and maintaining a conceptual focus. Other kinds of topics are no less promising, but they can be problematic in different ways:

- Concepts undergoing change: Some concepts may be treated from a static and historical perspective. For example, the concept of musical harmony can be considered to be stable and fixed. It might appear this way if one researched it only through reference sources and books. On the other hand, if one researched extensively in specialized periodicals, one could discover challenges by avant-garde musicians to traditional concepts of harmony. In this case, either treatment seems justified, depending on the purpose and audience. For other concepts, however, acknowledgment of recent developments and rapidly evolving trends seems vital to an accurate portrayal of the concept; notions of mental illness and democracy, for example, have undergone major transformations in recent years.

- Concepts about controversial issues: If your course will cover both explanatory writing (Chapter 5) and persuasive writing (Chapters 6–9), now is the time to begin discussing with your students the differences between the two genres. For this essay, we emphasize that their opinion should not be foregrounded or obviously stated, though it will certainly guide their selection and presentation of material. Students who have chosen a concept they have strong feelings about, for example, racism or recycling, will need your guidance to help them shape a balance, informative treatment of the topic, rather than a partisan, argumentative one.

- Concepts about personal life: Some students may be attracted to concepts for which personal experience will be their sole resource. Topics in this category from the Practicing Explaining Concepts: A Collaborative Activity section early in the chapter include romantic love, body image, and role model. Students may be more likely to choose these topics if the class has already done personal experience writing (Chapters 2 and 4). While this focus is certainly valid, you may choose to discourage it if other students will be developing concepts in ways that move beyond personal experience to involve published sources. Your guidance here can be supportive and enlightening: many students will be surprised to discover that library sources are available on such concepts as romance and body image, and that material from these sources may be interwoven with personal experience anecdotes to create an effective essay.

We recommend reviewing students' topic choices. They can't succeed at this assignment unless they've made appropriate topic choices.

Chapter 6 EVALUATION

This is a pivotal chapter in the book, the first that deals with argument. The preceding chapters introduced types of personal and explanatory discourse. In this chapter, students encounter discourse that makes and defends value judgments. Evaluation is one of the basic elements of argument, and students will need to recognize evaluative arguments in the remaining chapters of the book. In essays conjecturing about causes or speculating about effects, for example, writers judge the relative value of alternative explanations or predictions. Similarly, writers of proposals evaluate alternative solutions, and any piece of writing that advances an opinion is built on value judgments. Evaluation, then, is at the heart of any argument. In this chapter, students learn to recognize value judgments and to examine the standards on which they are based.

This chapter begins with a discussion of evaluations students make every day and suggests academic and other occasions for evaluative writing. The purpose here is to remind students that they already know something about evaluative discourse—when and why evaluations are written as well as by and to whom. This chapter builds on and refines what they already know.

The introduction also draws a distinction between expressions of taste and evaluations. Students could explore this distinction by defining terms such as *taste, preference,* and *judgment,* and by conjecturing about the different purposes of expressing, explaining, justifying, and convincing. The main point here is to help students classify evaluation as argumentative discourse.

WRITING ASSIGNMENT: Evaluation
This is the writing assignment that appears near the beginning of Chapter 6:

Write an essay, evaluating a particular subject. State your judgment clearly, and back it up with reasons and evidence. Describe the subject for readers unfamiliar with it, and give them a context for understanding it. Your principal aim is to convince readers that your judgment is informed and your reasons are based on generally accepted standards for judging this kind of subject.

For this general assignment, many specific topics are possible. Suggested topics (Considering Ideas for Your Own Writing) follow each reading, and there is a list of topic possibilities as part of the Invention section in the Guide to Writing an Evaluation.

Evaluative Writing Situations

The three writing situations early in the chapter illustrate a wide range of evaluations, academic and otherwise. The first two are clear negative evaluations, one academic and one on the job. Each demonstrates the characteristics mentioned in the writing assignment, presenting a definitive judgment, backing it up with sound reasons, and supporting these with specific evidence. The third situation, in which a college student evaluates colleges for his younger brother, does not highlight judgment quite as prominently; the writer narrows his choice to two colleges and then provides criteria by which his brother might make his own judgment. This example might be useful in introducing the role of comparison in evaluative writing.

Practicing Evaluation: A Collaborative Activity

This group activity is designed to engage students in the most basic and yet most difficult aspect of evaluative writing: choosing appropriate standards. Notice that the activity has two parts. First, students discuss the standards they would use for evaluating the kind of entertainment they have chosen and select the three they agree are most important. Then, they reflect on the process of choosing standards. The second part of the task will likely be new for them because few students—indeed few people other than experts in a field—think about the standards by which they judge things. Normally we just make judgments without thinking seriously about the values underlying our judgments. Through this group activity, you can lead students to recognize the importance of self-reflection and critical analysis. They will find the activity valuable in itself as well as for its rhetorical effectiveness.

If students have difficulty coming up with standards, you might advise them to think of a particular instance with which they are all familiar and to consider how they would judge that. The group activity asks them to arrive ultimately at a consensus about the two or three most important standards they might apply to a particular form of entertainment. But the process of consensus building often involves argument. They should also expect to disagree, and this activity will help them see how such disagreement can help them anticipate and handle the rhetorical situation in which they will be writing.

A GUIDE TO READING EVALUATIVE WRITING

This section once again leads students through the critical reading and writing strategies they will use throughout the chapter. For class activities to be used in conjunction with this section, see Part 5 of this manual.

Following a brief illustration of annotation, a sample essay by Amitai Etzioni clearly demonstrates the central features of evaluative writing: presenting the subject, asserting an overall judgment, giving reasons and supporting evidence, and establishing credibility. The Reading like a Writer section following the essay will break these down into specific strategies.

Reading for Meaning

As in each chapter, the first set of questions and suggestions following the sample essay are designed to help students focus closely on the text, exploring in writing their understanding of Etzioni's essay. We begin by asking students to summarize Etzioni's argument and identify his judgment of his topic. Students are also invited to reflect on their own work experience in relation to Etzioni's argument. This section, like the corresponding sections following each of the readings in the chapter, is likely to generate a wide range of responses as students find their own meanings in the text; students may need to be reminded that there is no "right" or "wrong" meaning.

Reading like a Writer

This section helps students shift their focus from the content of the essay to how the writer presents his evaluation—from reading exclusively as readers to reading as prospective writers. Students are introduced here to the major elements of evaluative writing: *presenting the subject, asserting an overall judgment, giving reasons and supporting evidence,* and *establishing credibility*. Through a series of brief critical reading and writing tasks, students focus on the strategies Etzioni, like other evaluative writers, uses to achieve each of these elements. Strategies for presenting the subject are discussed specifically, as are strategies for asserting a judgment. We then call attention to the important role of reasons and supporting evidence in presenting an evaluative argument; finally, we help students see that Etzioni establishes credibility both by projecting authority and by implying a bond of shared standards or values with his readers.

While the Reading like a Writer section following the sample essay presents a full range of strategies for evaluative writing, corresponding sections following each of the subsequent readings in the chapter will focus more narrowly on one or two strategies particularly appropriate to the analysis of each essay.

Presenting the Subject. Students will notice that Etzioni derives his information about his subject from a combination of sources, citing "studies" in his second paragraph, but also clearly relying largely on first- and secondhand observation of his subject. Students may point out that Etzioni's portrayal of the typical fast-food restaurant is rather extreme, conjuring up images of Orwellian automatons—hardly the image students are likely to have of themselves or their former selves and peers. Many students may be bothered by his tone; some will pinpoint the source of their discomfort in the fact that, regardless of his final exhortation to "go back to school," Etzioni is primarily writing not to the teenage "victims" of McDonald's but to their parents—and that, in fact, he seems undecided as to whether teenagers *are* in fact victims, or whether they're at best lazy and irresponsible, at worst criminals.

Asserting an Overall Judgment. Students should note that, while Etzioni's judgment is stated emphatically at the very beginning of the essay, it is restated in slightly different forms throughout the selection. For instance, at the end of paragraph 11, he aims his thesis specifically toward "minority youngsters." Students are also asked to consider whether Etzioni modifies his judgment at any point. You might guide students to see how acknowledging both good and bad qualities about a subject serves to make an evaluative argument more powerful.

Giving Reasons and Supporting Evidence. This task asks students to analyze and evaluate one of Etzioni's reasons for his judgment, along with the evidence he offers in support of that reason. Students are asked to consider the reason's appropriateness to Etzioni's overall argument, and then to judge the reliability of the supporting evidence. Once again, students may find that the three reasons from which the task asks them to choose—that fast-food jobs are too "routinized," that these jobs interfere with education, and that on-the-job supervision is inadequate or inappropriate—seem calculated to appeal not to teenagers or students, but to their parents. Students may also be critical of the evidence on which Etzioni draws to support these reasons. While the evidence of long hours and late closing times seem plausible in support of the second reason, the evidence in support of Etzioni's claims about routinization and supervision may strike students as being exaggerated, condescending, or both.

Establishing Credibility. This task asks students to examine the ways in which Etzioni invites readers' confidence in his judgment, and to evaluate the extent to which he is successful in maintaining his credibility. Students may note that Etzioni's authority derives from three areas: his own educational and professional background as a sociologist and researcher, the firsthand experience of his teenage sons, and his reference to various studies of the issue. Once again, students should note that, although Etzioni draws statistical material in support of his argument from these studies (two-thirds of American high schoolers work part time; minorities represent 21 percent of fast-food workers), he rejects the conclusions suggested in each study. Students may find that Etzioni's confidence in refuting these conclusions—presumably reached by experts—enhances their sense of his own authority. Also, as establishing credibility depends in large part on referring to standards or values with which readers will be able to identify, we encourage students to consider the values underlying Etzioni's judgment; most will recognize his invocation of the work ethic and self-reliance.

RESOURCES FOR TEACHING THE READINGS

The selections in this chapter offer evaluations in a range of fields including cinema, sports, literature, computer science, and the environment, offering students a sense of the broad scope of this genre. David Ansen's review of the movie *Quiz Show* is followed by Roger Angell's evaluation of the 1993 World Series; then comes Martha C. Nussbaum's essay on William Bennett's *Book of Virtues*. The pseudonymous Scorpia offers her evaluation of the computer game Menzoberranzan, followed by student Ilene Wolf's evaluation of an environmental magazine.

These essays demonstrate the essential characteristics of good evaluative writing. From them, students learn that writers of evaluations define their subjects clearly and provide readers with information about them; make value judgments about the subjects, base these judgments on appropriate standards, and support them with reasons and evidence. Students can also see that writers of reviews and other kinds of evaluative discourse must know a good deal about their subjects, but they often write for audiences who lack this knowledge. Writers therefore must find ways to inform their readers sufficiently so that they will be able to follow the argument.

The material that follows introduces each reading and offers advice for using the sections on reading for meaning and reading like a writer and the ideas for writing that follow each reading selection.

David Ansen, **When America Lost Its Innocence—Maybe**

This piece introduces a type of evaluation—the review—important within and outside the university. The film, released in 1994, is a powerful movie on an important subject that will be sure to elicit stimulating class discussion. Many of your students may have seen the movie; if not, you might consider showing it in class. Reading Ansen's evaluation after seeing and discussing the film will help students grasp the rhetorical situation in which the review was written; understanding the rhetorical situation will help them understand how evaluative writing, like all writing, is bound by its social context.

Reading for Meaning

This section helps students focus closely on the text, rereading and adding annotations as they develop their understanding. We ask students to write briefly as part of this activity; especially as this is the first reading selection in the chapter, you might want to collect their written responses and skim them quickly, not only to get a sense of how well they are understanding the reading, but also to read aloud a few of the more thoughtful responses.

<u>Extending Meaning through Conversation</u>. Once students have explored the meaning of each piece on their own, we ask them to share their insights with one or two other students in order to expand their understanding of the reading. Particularly following the first reading in each chapter, you might ask one student from each group to report briefly on a meaning, idea, or insight at which the group arrived during their discussion, a facet of the reading that extended the meanings each had come up with on his or her own. You could then lead a brief class discussion of how this group activity functions in the critical reading of the selections.

Reading like a Writer: Presenting the Subject

Before they begin this section, you might refer students back to the corresponding section on Presenting the Subject following the sample essay by Amitai Etzioni earlier in this chapter, where we point out that, in the act of naming and describing their subjects, writers often also indicate at least implicit value judgments. Here, students are asked to focus on the ways in which Ansen's very description of his subject suggests a certain judgment: the task of an evaluative writer is to both inform and convince, and the two are often combined.

Especially in the case of this first selection in the chapter, you could lead students through the Analyze section of this activity as a class, perhaps beginning by steering their attention toward the passage at the end of paragraph 5 beginning "It's about . . ." Students should be able to see how, in his description of the movie, Ansen incorporates what he feels to be its larger political messages. In leading students through the Analyze section, you can show them how to do a thorough analysis of a text, continuing to reread and annotate; once students have written their responses to this activity, you might invite them to share their writing in class.

Considering Ideas for Your Own Writing

This section asks students to consider writing movie reviews of their own. It invites them to rehearse the composing process by making the kinds of decisions they will need to make when they actually write their evaluative essays: choosing and presenting their topics and determining reasons for their judgments,

This is a challenging activity, one that you might want to support by taking class time to discuss their tentative decisions in small groups or with the whole class. You might consider grouping students according to current films they've seen and allow them to debate their evaluations.

Roger Angell, **Oh, What a Lovely War**

This selection moves away from the movie review to a type of evaluation perhaps equally familiar to many students: the sports review. Angell's evaluation of the 1993 World Series helps students to see that sportswriting need not be simply a play-by-play, statistics-filled report, but can actually make for lively and informative reading.

Reading for Meaning

Students are learning that perhaps the most important challenge facing the writer of an evaluation is to provide reasons for his or her judgment. We begin this activity by asking students to identify the reasons supporting Angell's positive judgment of the 1993 Series; in order to help students accomplish this part of the activity, you might need to remind them once again of the importance of rereading and annotating each text.

Extending Meaning through Conversation. Once again, we ask students to develop their understanding of the selection by discussing it with one or two other students. In this case, you may find that your students have a wide range of responses to sports-related topics, ranging from the completely uninterested to the fanatical. You can help them begin on common ground by calling their attention to our suggestion that they begin by focusing on Angell's seemingly oxymoronic title; you might further ensure that conversation continues to be fruitful by circulating among groups, offering suggestions and facilitating discussion.

Reading like a Writer: Asserting an Overall Judgment

This section should help students to see that although many writers of evaluation present their judgments clearly toward the beginning of their essays, others embed their judgments throughout the text, as Angell does. You may need to help students see that Angell's judgment of the 1993 Series is suggested at both the beginning and the the end of the first paragraph, and then developed at the beginnings of the third and fifth paragraphs. We call students' attention to the use of value terms; you might point out that these often appear in the form of adjectives, as in the case of Angell's characterization of the Series as "excessive and astounding."

Compare. This important activity, which follows one or two of the readings in each chapter, helps students see how different writers use the same strategies. In this case, we ask students to compare Angell's use of value terms to Etzioni's or Ansen's use of such terms. Students may note that Angell's terms, like those of many sportswriters, tend to be highly colorful (as in "grisly or glorious" in paragraph 1) if not hyperbolic. Once students have completed this activity, you might invite them to share their responses briefly in class.

Considering Ideas for Your Own Writing

Here, we invite students to consider evaluating a sports-related topic. Whether students think about evaluating an event, team, or sports figure, you may need to remind them that, in addition to establishing standards by which their potential readers are likely to judge such subjects, they will need to present concrete evidence of how their subject does or does not measure up to such standards.

Martha C. Nussbaum, **Divided We Stand**

Here we move from movie reviews and sportswriting to a third, and probably equally familiar, type of evaluation: the book review. Students are likely to find Nussbaum's essay particularly challenging, rich with references and sophisticated vocabulary, so you might plan on spending some extra class time to guide them through it.

Reading for Meaning

We ask students to begin by paraphrasing Nussbaum's judgment of Bennett's book; you might take a moment to remind students of the value of paraphrasing in making meaning from a text. Once students have completed the Reading for Meaning section, you could ask a few of them to share their responses in class, both as a way of encouraging discussion of the piece and as a way for you to monitor how well they are understanding this somewhat difficult reading.

Extending Meaning through Conversation. As students develop their understanding of this selection in conversation with one or two of their classmates, you may find that you need to supervise the pairs or groups fairly closely, answering questions about the text and helping students stay focused on Nussbaum's judgment. Once students have completed this activity, you could have one member of each group report briefly to the class on a meaning arrived at by the group that extended the meanings students had found separately.

Contextualizing (A Further Strategy for Reading for Meaning). Periodically throughout the text, at least once in each chapter, we refer students to the supplemental critical reading strategies presented in Appendix 1 of the text. In this case, we are inviting students to develop their understanding of the meaning of the reading selection in a very specific historical and political context. You might help them to get started with this activity by referring them to the headnote introducing the piece.

Reading like a Writer: Establishing Credibility

Students should have little trouble noting that Nussbaum is obviously well read; they should also appreciate that she brings not only her academic background but also her personal experience to bear on her evaluation of Bennett's book. This activity also draws students' attention to the crucial issue of *balance* in evaluations. You might take a few minutes of class time to preview this idea for students by asking them to consider whether, as readers, they would be more likely to be convinced, on the one hand, by a review that was either completely positive, acknowledging none of the weaknesses in its subject, or completely negative, acknowledging none of its subject's strong points, or, on the other hand, by a review that presented both the strengths and the weaknesses of its subject, and then made a thoughtful case for either a positive or a negative judgment.

Compare. As students continue to analyze and write about Nussbaum's piece, they will find it useful to compare it to other selections in the chapter. If students have trouble getting started on this activity, you might suggest that they compare Nussbaum's evaluation to the sample essay by Amitai Etzioni, perhaps approaching their comparison by commenting on how much balance each writer achieves in what is basically a negative evaluation of his or her topic.

Considering Ideas for Your Own Writing

We do not personally wish to encourage moral evaluation, but students might learn how it differs from other standards of judgment by doing a brief moral evaluation of a poem or short short story you have copied for them and then doing another brief evaluation based on other standards.

Scorpia, **Beware of the Under Drow**

The inclusion of this selection in the textbook helps to remind students that evaluations are often highly specialized. While some of your students are very likely to be familiar with computer role-playing games, many are not; you might open a discussion of this piece by taking an informal survey of your class to see which students are familiar or unfamiliar with the subject, and then by asking them to be particularly aware of how this affects their understanding as they read the essay.

Reading for Meaning

As usual, we ask students to begin this activity by putting the writer's judgment in their own words. Most students will have no trouble recognizing that, although Scorpia acknowledges both strong and weak points in her subject, her overall judgment is negative, as expressed at the beginnings of paragraphs 7 and 19. As students proceed through this activity, remind them of the importance of rereading and annotating in making meaning from a text.

Extending Meaning through Conversation. If you have introduced this selection by asking which students are familiar with this type of computer game and which are not, you might try to arrange pairs or groups so that each includes at least one student who has some experience with the subject. Keep students focused on the essay itself by moving from group to group, calling students' attention to the selection as an example of evaluative writing.

Reading like a Writer: Giving Reasons

By now, students should understand that writers of evaluation need to offer specific reasons in support of their judgments. Once students identify what Scorpia sees as the one strength (the auto-mapping system) and the two major weaknesses of this game (that its setup is too linear and that it has programming problems), they should be able to analyze the reasons Scorpia offers in support of these assertions. Once students have completed this activity, you might invite a few of them to share their responses in class.

Considering Ideas for Your Own Writing

Computer-related topics offer a wealth of possibilities for students planning their own evaluative essays. You could remind students here that they will need to consider their audience carefully, deciding whether they are writing for readers who are novices, computer experts, or merely moderately computer-literate.

Ilene Wolf, Buzzworm: **The Superior Magazine**

As they read this final selection in this chapter, written by student Ilene Wolf, students should note her use of comparison and contrast, as well as her standards for judgment.

Reading for Meaning

This section asks students to focus closely on the text, clarifying their impressions of the magazine *Buzzworm*, as well as their understanding of Wolf's evaluation of her subject. Students should find this essay accessible and interesting, and should have little trouble commenting on its meaning.

Extending Meaning through Conversation. Here, as usual, we invite students to develop their understanding of the selection by discussing it with one or two other students. You may find that students are somewhat uncritically accepting of Wolf's views; our suggestions that they examine some of the assumptions underlying her evaluation should help students broaden their own and each others' perspectives.

Reading like a Writer: Supporting Reasons with Examples

This section highlights the role of specific examples in supporting evaluative arguments. Students will have little difficulty identifying Wolf's use of examples in support of her judgment. Students should also note that Wolf's essay revolves around her comparison and contrast of two magazines, *Buzzworm* and *Sierra*, and that her extensive use of specific examples from each help make her evaluation more convincing. Some students may point out that the element of contrast is missing in paragraph 4, perhaps weakening the effect of the specific examples cited in that paragraph.

Reading like a Writer: A Follow-up Activity

As students complete the Reading like a Writer activities in each chapter, they should review the considerable amount of writing they have generated in response to the reading selections. They may be surprised at how much they have learned about the genre. You might ask students to choose one piece of their own writing to revise and expand; they would turn this piece in with their final essay packages or with their end-of-course portfolios.

Considering Ideas for Your Own Writing

This section invites students to consider writing their own evaluations of written works, and to begin to consider the standards by which they would judge a magazine, newspaper, essay, story, poem, or book. Depending on your own assessment of the Wolf essay, you might wish to point out to students using it as a model that, though it is undeniably a good essay, it does not necessarily represent a pinnacle of achievement in student writing.

THINKING ABOUT WHAT MAKES EVALUATION EFFECTIVE

As in each chapter in the text, we ask students to reflect on the reading and writing they have done, reviewing and consolidating what they have learned about each genre. You can ensure that students get the most out of this activity by making sure they look back at the four basic features of evaluative writing (presenting the subject, asserting a judgment, giving reasons and supporting evidence, and establishing credibility) as they are presented in A Guide to Reading Evaluative Writing early in the chapter.

A GUIDE TO WRITING AN EVALUATION

The guide leads students through a composing process that follows these steps:

Invention
    Choosing a Subject
    Exploring Your Subject
    Analyzing Your Readers
        Learning More About Your Readers: A Collaborative Activity
    Considering Your Judgment
    Listing Reasons
    Finding Evidence to Support Your Reasons
    Drawing Comparisons
Drafting
    Setting Goals
    Planning Your Draft
    Beginning
    Avoiding Logical Fallacies
Reading a Draft Critically
    Reading for a First Impression
    Reading to Analyze
        Presentation of the Subject
        Statement of the Overall Judgment
        Supporting Reasons and Evidence
        Credibility
Revising
    Revising to Present the Subject
    Revising to Clarify the Overall Judgment
    Revising to Strengthen the Reasons and Evidence
Reflecting on What You Have Learned about Writing Evaluation

Topic choice is a crucial step for all students, and a difficult step for many. You might ask students to bring to class a list of possible subjects they might evaluate, and devote some class time to discussing these topics in small groups. Or you might ask the whole class to brainstorm a list of potential topics. By sharing potential topics with their classmates, students will discover which are of immediate interest to others. They will also get a sense of which subjects require extended description and what standards are generally applied to them. Other students' ideas will probably also inspire those who are having difficulty choosing a subject.

From studying the readings, students should grasp the importance of providing enough information about a subject to enable readers to follow an evaluative argument about it. Students also need to anticipate any prejudices in their readers they may have to overcome. Pairs of students might rehearse their arguments and refutations to counterarguments with each other. These dialogues should help students imagine how other readers might respond to their argument.

In setting goals, students should reconsider the larger rhetorical issues of purpose and audience before planning their organization. Often, inexperienced writers get stuck because they feel there is one right way to begin or to organize an essay. It is important for writers to view drafting more flexibly and to consider their decisions in terms appropriate to their particular aims and the needs of their readers.

SPECIAL PROBLEMS OF THIS WRITING ASSIGNMENT. This seems like a straightforward assignment: say whether you like or dislike something, and then say why. It can, nevertheless, go wrong in many ways the first time student writers try it. Students may not be willing to assert firm judgments, or they may not understand—even after the readings and Reading like a Writer activities in the text—that they are to make and defend by reasoned argument their own judgments. In addition, because they are unaccustomed to being held to the rhetorical requirements of a specific writing situation, student writers may overlook the requirement to describe the subject for readers who are unfamiliar with it. They may also unwittingly merge or blur their reasons because they lack confidence in them. Likewise, they may underestimate how well they grasp the standards for evaluating a particular subject or assume standards are generally shared when they are not.

These problems suggest that before you ask students to analyze each other's drafts, you may want to lead a class discussion of two or three drafts. During this discussion, you can insist firmly that the writers meet the rhetorical requirements of the assignment. Furthermore, the problems of the assignment make the evaluation a good choice for a double assignment in which you ask students immediately to do a second essay on a different subject. For the first essay, you could give them two or three choices of subjects, such as the same story or movie, and then they could choose their own subjects for the second essay.

Perhaps the biggest problem of all arises when students risk doing this assignment from memory. A subject to be evaluated needs to be studied and restudied before and during invention and drafting. Students should not evaluate a movie unless they can see it two or three times, nor should they evaluate a novel unless they have time to reread it. Likewise, they should not evaluate a consumer product unless they are currently using it.

Evaluation essays are so well understood, their features so well established, that we can hold students to a standard of performance that may startle them in its fullness and precision.

PROMISING AND UNPROMISING TOPICS. The first step in the Invention section for this chapter asks students to list possible subjects for their evaluation essays. We provide a list of general topic areas to get students started, a list drawn from our own experience with successful and unsuccessful topics. As you can see, we suggest a range of possible topic areas—including media, arts, literature, education, government, campus, and leisure—that extends far beyond the few examples we have provided through the chapter readings. Though each item on this list is a potentially fruitful source of ideas for evaluation topics, each item nevertheless poses its own peculiar problems and dangers. You may wish to narrow down this list for your own students and preclude certain topics.

Our experience has shown us that the most successful essays are those that draw heavily on an individual student's interest or expertise. Students who express an avid interest in skateboarding often write fine essays on skateboard magazines, skateboard parks, or skateboard models. Not only are they familiar with the standards that are usually applied to that field of interest, but they have also been able to make comparisons and contrasts to related subjects (for example, other skateboard magazines, parks, or models) with some ease. The topics themselves can be quite ambitious—we have had some remarkable essays evaluating such things as strategic nuclear arms treaties and UAW contracts—but they are successful only when the student has either a fair amount of expertise or a deep interest in the topic itself. You should, by all means, encourage your students to draw on their own strengths, knowledge base, and interests when choosing topics.

By and large, students have the least amount of difficulty evaluating consumer products. Standards are fairly easy to establish, the essays themselves are not difficult to structure and control, and comparisons can often be found in personal experience or a recent issue of *Consumer Reports*. Still, there are some significant dangers in permitting students to write essays of this type. Students all too often have a tendency to slip into a kind of Madison Avenue prose, uncritically touting the virtues of their chosen product and making claims of "comfort" or "style" that are unsupported by any kind of evidence. Trivial criteria and matters of personal taste can run rampant in evaluations of consumer products, and students should be warned about such flaws in advance. We discourage essays about consumer products, and some instructors forbid them.

Evaluations of people are also likely to be successful as long as students are careful to establish clear and reasonable standards and show some awareness that no one is perfect (or perfectly bad). Generally speaking, the worst topic choices are people with whom the writer is too emotionally involved. Teachers are a popular topic for evaluation, but watch out for essays that lapse into simple narratives or make claims ("He was a friend to his students as well as a teacher . . .") without any kind of support.

We are also wary of topics that try to evaluate abstract concepts such as "friendship" or "greed." Though it is theoretically possible to write such evaluations, it is extremely difficult to decide upon appropriate standards. Even more difficult is determining the kind of evidence that might be brought to bear on such a topic. Our students have occasionally written credible essays evaluating "capitalism" or "democracy," but the key to their success seems to lie in the fact that these concepts can be illustrated by referring to specific examples (for example, the United States, Great Britain). Evaluations of philosophical abstractions almost always lead to more problems than rewards.

Easily the most promising topics are discrete, tangible objects or events that can be revisited and analyzed—a story or novel, movie, musical recording, concert, play performance, essay in this book, magazine, restaurant, college program or service. Before drafting, students can revisit the subject, taking careful notes. They can revisit once again before revising, keeping the subject *present* throughout the writing process. Such immediate presence of the subjects makes it easier for students to amass the evidence or examples required in a strong evaluation essay.

Chapter 7 SPECULATION ABOUT CAUSES OR EFFECTS

This is the second in a series of three closely related chapters dealing with important types of argument or persuasion. In Chapter 6, students learned about the basic building block of argument—value judgment. This chapter introduces them to causal argument—argument about the influence of one thing on another when the nature of this influence is not clear. Since this kind of argumentation concerns explanation and prediction, it is a crucial mode of inquiry and writing in the sciences and social sciences.

Arguments about causes or effects in turn become important elements in proposals, the topic of Chapter 8, as writers use these arguments to explain what has caused a problem, what its effects will be if no solution is found, and what effects each possible solution is likely to have.

In discussing the introduction to this chapter, you should help students see that the focus is on analysis and argument—on conjecture and speculation about possible causes or effects of events, trends, or phenomena. The selections do not simply summarize uncritically others' proposed causes or effects but argue inventively for the writers' own proposed causes or effects for a subject that cannot presently (or perhaps ever) be explained definitively or scientifically. The students' essays will also present such speculative arguments. Students may very well research other proposed causes or effects for their topic, but not in order to collect and summarize these causes or effects in the essay. Instead, they will weigh and evaluate each cause or effect, analyzing it in light of their understanding of the topic and the argument they want to make. Students must argue for their preferred causes or effects, whether they discovered them on their own or turned them up in their research.

WRITING ASSIGNMENT: Speculating about Causes or Effects

Here is the writing assignment that appears near the beginning of Chapter 7:

> Choose a subject that invites you to speculate about its causes or effects—why it might have happened or what its effects may be. Write an essay, arguing for your proposed causes or effects. Essays about causes look to the past to ponder why something happened, whereas essays about effects guess what is likely to happen in the future. Whether you are writing an essay about causes or effects, you need to do two things: (1) establish the existence and significance of the subject (an event, a phenomenon, or a trend) and (2) convince readers that the causes or effects you propose are plausible.

This writing assignment is both challenging and satisfying for students. It helps them develop their powers of creativity as they speculate about possible causes or effects, their powers of judgment as they weigh the possibilities and choose the most plausible ones, and their powers of reasoning as they devise an argumentative strategy to present their conclusions to readers. The assignment is presented in generic terms, and possible topics are listed following each reading (Considering Ideas for Your Own Writing) and in the Invention section of the Guide to Writing. You may wish to limit the range of possible topics (see Special Problems of this Writing Assignment, below).

Cause or Effect Writing Situations

The three writing situations presented early in the chapter demonstrate that writers analyze and explain the causes and effects of events, phenomena, and trends in both academic and non-academic settings. The three situations also illustrate two important decisions students will make as they begin to consider writing their own essays: first, whether to write about causes or effects, and second, whether to write about events, phenomena, or trends. The first writing situation examines the causes of a phenomenon (which students may note might also have been treated as a trend); the second speculates about causes of a trend, and the third analyzes the effects of a subject that could be treated as either phenomenon or trend. These situations will inform students about the essay they will be writing, especially if you discuss the situations with them, emphasizing both the particular decisions the writers had to make and the unique features of this kind of writing.

Practicing Speculation about Causes or Effects: A Collaborative Activity

This activity is designed to engage students in making the kinds of decisions they will make as writers about causes or effects. In the first part of the activity, students are asked to decide as a group on an event, a phenomenon, or a trend, and then to speculate briefly about its causes or effects. In the second part of the activity, students are asked to reflect on and discuss the process of cause-and-effect speculation. Students may need help making the shift between the first and second parts of the activity.

A GUIDE TO READING SPECULATION ABOUT CAUSES OR EFFECTS

This section leads students through the critical reading and writing strategies they will use throughout the chapter. For class activities to be used in conjunction with this section, see Part 5 of this manual.

The sample essay provided in this section, following a brief illustration of annotation, clearly demonstrates the central features of writing about causes or effects: presenting the subject, making a cause or effect argument, handling objections and alternative causes or effects, and establishing credibility. The Reading like a Writer section following the essay will break these down into more specific strategies.

Stephen King's essay on the phenomenon of the appeal of horror movies has the advantages of a quick pace and a familiar topic—nearly everyone has squirmed through at least one horror film. Because students' attitudes toward horror movies are likely to vary from repulsion to indifference to the "craving" noted by King, this essay can introduce a discussion of how different readers may react to the same argument. King's essay also illustrates how moving from obvious causes to deeper or "hidden" causes is a convincing argumentative strategy, and how an expressive personal voice is appropriate in some argumentative writing situations.

Reading for Meaning

As usual, this section asks for students' general reactions to the content of the selection, inviting them to explore their understanding of and response to Stephen King's essay. Students are invited to speculate about King's assumptions regarding his audience, and to delve further into some of the issues raised in King's argument. You might use students' responses to this section as the basis for class discussion; the section is designed to stimulate students' interest in the reading and to increase the likelihood that they will want to analyze it closely.

Reading like a Writer

Here, students move from examining the content or ideas in the essay to analyzing the features of this type of writing and the specific strategies used by the writer. This work directly anticipates the thinking they will do as they read the other selections in the chapter and as they plan and draft their own essays. This section introduces students to the major elements of writing about causes and effects: *presenting the subject, making a cause or effect argument, handling objections and alternative causes or effects,* and *establishing credibility.* Students will examine how King establishes the existence and significance of his subject; they will also focus on King's causal argument: the ways in which he proposes possible causes, constructs a plausible argument, and handles objections and alternative explanations. Finally, students will examine how—or whether—King establishes credibility by gaining the confidence and respect of his readers.

The Reading like a Writer section following the sample essay presents a full range of strategies for writing about causes or effects. Corresponding sections following each of the subsequent reading selections in the chapter will focus more closely on one or two strategies particularly appropriate to the analysis of each essay. You may want to remind students that, while there are technically no "right" or "wrong" responses to this section, students are accountable for the depth and precision of their engagement with specific aspects of the text.

Presenting the Subject. Students will notice that King presents his subject as a phenomenon, rather than as an event or a trend. This is a good opportunity to discuss how presenting the subject may be weighted somewhat differently depending on whether the subject is an event, a phenomenon, or a trend: in general, establishing the existence of an event or a phenomenon is relatively simple, while suggesting its significance may be somewhat more difficult; in the case of a trend, students will be challenged both to establish the existence of a trend and its significance. Students should note that King seems to assume that the existence of his phenomenon is a foregone conclusion, and that he suggests its significance in part through his claim that all humans share a kind of generic insanity, and that horror movies provide a safety release valve that is relatively harmless compared with the alternatives King implies in his mention of serial murderers and psychopaths.

Making a Cause or Effect Argument. Students will note first of all that King focuses on the causes rather than the effects of the phenomenon in question; they should also note that he proposes three main causes for the popularity of horror movies, ranging from (1) the "simple and obvious" fact that such movies allow viewers to prove to others—and to themselves—that they "are not afraid," to (2) the idea that horror movies help maintain our sense of the normal, to (3) the claim that these movies provide a specific type of "fun." While some students may find King's second proposed cause—that even the most extreme horror films are perversely reassuring—the most sophisticated and intriguing, they will note that King's discussion glosses over this cause in favor of his third and final proposed cause. His rather provocative thesis that the "fun" of horror movies functions as a necessary antidote to our shared insanity is foreshadowed in his first paragraph. In expanding on a seemingly obvious cause, "having fun," King develops his proposed cause, a hidden cause with deeper implications: We go to horror movies, he argues, to at once exercise and control emotions that might be harmful to society if released. It is worth noting that, although King's essay focuses primarily on *causes*, his proposed *cause* for the popularity of horror movies is based on the psychological *effect* of the movies themselves.

As students continue to analyze and write briefly about King's argument, we invite them to examine its plausibility, focusing on his use of analogy. In particular, students are asked to analyze very closely and write briefly about his analogy between viewing horror movies and riding roller coasters. Students are then encouraged to extend this analysis to King's analogies of horror films to football games and "sick jokes."

Handling Objections and Alternative Causes or Effects. In a sense, King's entire essay is planned to refute objections: its argumentative stance is clear from the first sentence. But it is not easy to pick out specific points at which King refutes a specific objection or counterargument. The objection most likely to occur to a student reader is this: "I enjoy horror movies, but I don't think I'm sick or insane." King anticipates this objection by asserting that "sanity" is, in fact, "a matter of degree." Students should also note that the "alternative explanations" King presents are not seen in opposition to his proposed main cause, and that King acknowledges and accommodates these alternatives.

Students are asked to comment in writing on King's handling of the objection implied in the rhetorical question "why bother?" (paragraph 13); they are also invited to pose other objections or questions. For instance, some students may note that King's somewhat glib treatment avoids the issue of the psychological and emotional effects of exposure to violence, whether real or cinematic.

Establishing Credibility. Students should recall from the evaluation assignment in Chapter 6 that writers of evaluations establish credibility by projecting authority and by establishing, or at least suggesting, a sense of shared values with their readers; and they should note that King's essay follows the same basic pattern. Since King is a well-known writer of horror novels, several of which have been made into movies, the reader is clearly expected to consider him an authoritative source. Students may or may not find this authority convincing on its own. They may ask why King's argument makes no reference to the large body of psychological or social science research on this subject; some may suggest that, given King's audience, such reference is neither necessary nor appropriate.

King attempts to build a bond with readers by linking his observations about human behavior to common actions most people have experienced or witnessed: "We've all known people who talk to themselves," we've all heard "sick jokes," most of us have experienced emotions that might be called "uncivilized. Recognition of these shared experiences, reflected in King's use of the first-person plural pronouns *we* and *us*, helps readers to accept King's credibility in presenting his argument.

Although King's conversational tone and familiar style seem engaging and believable for many readers, students may challenge King's authority on a number of points: He is not an expert in psychology or social science, nor does he quote any such expert; he does not unequivocally refute objections and alternative causes; his own proposed cause is highly speculative. Astute readers may also want to examine the possible connections between the fact that King's audience is the readers of *Playboy* and the fact that both the victims and the much-tried "survivors" of most horror movies tend to be young women.

RESOURCES FOR TEACHING THE READINGS

The readings in this chapter cover a range of events, phenomena, and trends. The sample essay by Stephen King critically examines the causes of the phenomenal popularity of horror movies. The four following essays also deal with social issues in the form of either phenomena or trends: Natalie Angier speculates about the causes of a trend of increased intolerance toward "boyish" behavior, while Andrew Greeley examines the causes of the phenomenon of Catholics remaining faithful to the Catholic church. Jonathan Kozol writes about the effects of the phenomenon of illiteracy in America, and Steven Waldman explores the effects of the trend toward a proliferation of choice. Student writer Reese Mason speculates about the causes of an "event": the decision by college basketball star Hank Gathers to risk his life by continuing to compete after a diagnosis of heart trouble.

These readings represent a range of different approaches to speculating about the causes or effects of things that have happened, are happening now, or may happen in the future. Across this range, students can identify the basic features of argumentative discourse in each of the essays: a clear definition and demonstration of the event, trend, or phenomenon; speculation about its causes or effects; and a consideration of alternative causes or effects—all presented to readers reasonably and authoritatively.

The material that follows introduces each reading and explores the possibilities in the sections on reading for meaning and reading like a writer and the ideas for writing that follow each reading.

Natalie Angier, **Intolerance of Boyish Behavior**

With this essay, we move from speculation about the causes of a phenomenon, as in Stephen King's piece, to an examination of the causes of a trend. You will need to make sure that students understand that a trend, unlike a phenomenon, is something that changes over time.

Reading for Meaning
This section asks students to reread the text closely, beginning by concentrating on Angier's presentation of the trend. For this first reading in the chapter, we suggest that you lead students through this activity as a class, making notes on the board as students explore the meaning of the text.

Extending Meaning through Conversation. Once you have explored the meaning of the text as a class, students can further develop their understanding of the piece by discussing it with one or two classmates. You may find that male and female students respond to this selection differently; be sure to invite them to explore these differences as a valuable way of making meaning from the text. Once students have completed this activity, you could set aside some class time to discuss how it went and what meanings were developed through group conversation.

Reading like a Writer: Handling Objections
Anticipating the concerns and objections of readers is a fundamental component of all argumentative writing; here, we help students to focus on this important aspect of writing about causes and effects. We draw students' attention to specific paragraphs in which Angier seems to respond to possible questions on the part of her readers. As students analyze and write about the ways in which Angier handles potential objections, they should begin considering how they will respond to readers' concerns in their own essays. Once again, for this first reading selection in the chapter, you could guide students through the analysis portion of the activity as a class, and then allow them to write briefly on their own before asking them to share their observations with the class.

Considering Ideas for Your Own Writing

Here, we ask students to consider speculating about trends in group behavior, a rich source of topic ideas for this assignment. This section invites students to practice the two main strategies they'll need to use if they decide to write about the causes of a trend: First, they will need to establish the existence of the trend (a crucial step that poses a real challenge for beginning writers); then they will propose a possible cause (or causes) of the trend. You might ask students to discuss their own experiences or observations in groups of three or four, and then open up the discussion to include the entire class, perhaps listing proposed possible causes on the board.

Andrew M. Greeley, **Why Do Catholics Stay in the Church? Because of the Stories**

Whatever your students' religious orientations, they are likely to enjoy Greeley's somewhat surprising explanation of the phenomenon of the faithfulness of Catholics to their church.

Reading for Meaning

We ask students to begin exploring the meaning of Greeley's essay by examining his audience and purpose, rereading and annotating in order to develop their understanding of the piece. We also ask students to refer to their own experience in making meaning from this piece; as religion is often a challenging topic for students to discuss objectively, you may want to handle this part of the activity as a class discussion, inviting students to share their opinions orally. In this way, you can help students make explicit connections between their experiences and the text, ensuring that students who are using their own experience to make meaning from the reading are not moving entirely away from the essay itself.

Extending Meaning through Conversation. As in each assignment in this textbook, we ask students to extend the meanings they develop on their own by discussing the reading selection with one or two classmates. To help students keep on track, you might want to move from group to group, offering suggestions and drawing their attention back to the text itself.

Recognizing the Emotional Appeal of an Argument (A Further Strategy for Reading for Meaning). Periodically throughout the text, we refer students to one of the supplemental critical reading strategies outlined in the first appendix. In this case, we ask students to examine the emotional appeal of Greeley's essay, commenting on whether they feel manipulated by his argument. Once they have written a few sentences, you could ask them to share their responses to this activity either in small groups or as a class; because some students are likely to feel strongly about religious topics, you may find that you need to guide their discussion.

Reading like a Writer: Making a Causal Argument through Examples

In this section, we guide students through a careful analysis of Greeley's argument. Before students start this activity, take the opportunity to remind them of the importance of close rereading and annotating in learning about the strategies different writers use. Once students have completed their analyses and written briefly in response to this activity, you could have them share their responses orally in class, keeping a list on the board of the examples students have identified in Greeley's essay.

Considering Ideas for Your Own Writing

Where we invited students to consider analyzing a trend in group behavior following the previous selection, here we ask them to think about examining the causes of a phenomenon in group behavior. If some of your students do choose to write about religious phenomena (or trends, for that matter), you may need to stress the importance of maintaining an appearance of objectivity, avoiding proselytizing.

Jonathan Kozol, **The Human Cost of an Illiterate Society**

The essays by King, Angier, and Greeley all examine causes. This essay by Kozol is the first of the readings that looks at effects—in this case, of a phenomenon. Kozol demonstrates the problem of illiteracy in the United States and explains the significance of illiteracy for individuals and for the nation, arguing that it is a moral problem that challenges the notion of democracy in America.

Reading for Meaning

This section directs the students back to the text, asking them to explore their understanding of Kozol's argument. Students are asked to focus specifically on Kozol's use of examples, and invited to comment on the persuasiveness of his argument. Once students have written briefly in response to our suggestions, you might ask a few students to share their writing orally in class as a way of generating discussion of the meaning of the piece.

Extending Meaning through Conversation. As students discuss the meanings they have found in Kozol's essay with one or two classmates, they may find that they have different understandings of the text. Students who have had difficulty with reading themselves, for instance, may find Kozol's argument especially compelling, as they are more easily able to empathize with Kozol's subject.

Reading like a Writer: Making an Effects Argument by Organizing and Sequencing Effects

Kozol mentions at least twenty results of illiteracy, but students will probably come up with varying numbers, because some of the results are clustered together. The point is not for students to determine the exact number of results, but to see that there are many, and that they may be interrelated and interdependent. Students may describe the effect of the enumeration as impressive—even overwhelming. Some may feel that Kozol gives more results than necessary to make his point; others may argue that readers need this comprehensive survey of everyday information most people take for granted, but which is beyond the reach of the illiterate, before they can appreciate the magnitude and seriousness of the problem. Once students have written brief evaluations of Kozol's presentation of possible effects, you might have them share their responses in small groups or with the class as a whole.

Considering Ideas for Your Own Writing

These writing ideas ask students to speculate on the effects of a social problem or a controversial decision made by community or college leaders. A key element in each assignment is students' personal involvement in the problem or decision. You might remind students of the effect of Kozol's involvement in the illiteracy problem on the tone of his essay;

you might also remind them that the writing suggestions call for argument, not just guesswork. Students will probably be able to point to present effects of the problem or decision as well as future ones.

Steven Waldman, **The Tyranny of Choice**

Waldman's humor and irony stand in strong contrast to the serious appeals of Kozol in the preceding selection in this chapter. Waldman catalogs the less than positive effects of the trend toward more and more choices. The introductory note to the selection asks students to consider briefly their own experience with making choices before reading Waldman's essay.

Reading for Meaning

This section asks students once again to connect their ideas directly to the essay, beginning by identifying and commenting on the effects they feel to be most convincing in Waldman's essay. Further suggestions invite students to focus closely on specific aspects of the text; once students have completed this activity, you could have them share their responses in class as a way of facilitating discussion of the piece.

Extending Meaning through Conversation. You might help students get started in their small-group discussions of this essay by suggesting that each student offer an example from his or her own experience of facing many choices. Be sure, however, that their conversations return to the essay itself, making explicit connections between the text and students' own experience.

Reading like a Writer: Presenting the Subject by Establishing the Trend

Like all writers speculating about the causes or effects of a trend, Waldman must first convince his readers that such a trend actually exists, and is not an ongoing phenomenon, an isolated event, or a superficial fad. This task asks students to analyze and write briefly about Waldman's presentation of the trend. Students should note that Waldman employs an effective combination of statistical material, citation of an authority, and personal anecdote in establishing the existence of the trend. You might ask students to consider the effect on Waldman's argument if he had relied solely either on statistics and authorities or on personal anecdotes.

Considering Ideas for Your Own Writing

Although Waldman's essay is somewhat humorous in tone, this section invites students to think seriously about such issues as commitment and political alienation. This is another good opportunity to discuss the differences between trends and phenomena, for instance, you might point out that political alienation could be treated either as an ongoing phenomenon or as a trend on the increase in our century. Students could also focus on either the causes or the effects of either the phenomenon or the trend. They need to see that these decisions, usually made early in the writing process, will have a significant effect on the overall approach they take to their own essays.

Reese Mason, **Basketball and the Urban Poor**

While Mason's title suggests that he might be writing about either a phenomenon or a trend, his essay actually addresses what might be called an event: the decision by basketball star Hank Gathers to continue to play after a medical diagnosis of heart problems, and Gathers's subsequent on-court death.

If your students have done or will do the reflection essay assignment presented in Chapter 4, you might point out that Mason's essay resembles a reflective essay in that it uses a particular "occasion" as a starting point.

Reading for Meaning

This section directs students back to the text, asking them to begin by identifying the causes the writer proposes. Students are also invited to examine their own reasons for attending college, as well as their own conceptions of the American Dream; these suggestions should provide a useful basis for class discussion, as well as for the following activity.

Extending Meaning through Conversation. As usual, we ask students to expand on the meanings they have made from the text on their own by discussing the essay with one or two other students. As the Reading for Meaning suggestions imply, students will very likely find their personal experience useful in making meaning from this particular text; you might circulate among groups to make sure conversations do not move entirely away from the essay itself.

Reading like a Writer: Establishing Credibility

Students will have little trouble understanding the importance of credibility in an argument essay. We ask the students to reread and annotate Mason's essay, identifying the methods by which Mason attempts to establish his own credibility and commenting on the success of these methods. Some students will find Mason's argument more or less credible than others; some, for instance, may be put off by Mason's use of generalizations and his evocation of the familiar—almost cliché—scenario of young African-American men pulling themselves up out of the inner cities by their Nike laces. Other students will not have even recognized this aspect of Mason's essay, or may not see it as a weakness.

Compare. As we do following one or two reading selections in each chapter, we ask students to develop their analyses of a piece by comparing it with another essay in the same chapter. In this case, we ask students to reread and annotate for Mason's and one other writer's attempts to establish credibility. You might help students get started by asking them whether Mason's use of the first person adds to or detracts from their sense of his credibility, and then asking them to consider the use of the first person by one of the other writers in the chapter (King, Greeley, or Waldman).

Reading like a Writer: A Follow-up Activity

As students complete this last Reading like a Writer activity in the chapter, they will have generated a substantial amount of writing in response to the selections in the text. To help them review and consolidate what they have learned about writing in this genre, we suggest that you have them choose one of their Reading like a Writer responses to revise and extend by doing further analysis. Students would turn this piece in with their final essay packages or in their end-of-course portfolios.

Considering Ideas for Your Own Writing

This section invites students to consider writing about phenomena, trends, or events in sports. You might need to remind students that, if they choose to examine a *trend* in sports, their first task will be to establish that the trend exists.

THINKING ABOUT WHAT MAKES SPECULATION ABOUT CAUSES OR EFFECTS EFFECTIVE

In this section, which follows the reading selections in each chapter, we remind students of the basic features—originally listed following the sample essay—of successful writing in each genre. By selecting the one essay from the chapter they feel to be the most effective, rereading and annotating it, and finally justifying their choices of essay, students develop and consolidate what they have learned about each type of writing. This activity helps students focus closely on the features of the genre as they embark on their own essays.

A GUIDE TO WRITING SPECULATION ABOUT CAUSES OR EFFECTS

The guide leads students through a composing process that follows these steps:

Invention
    Choosing a Subject
    Exploring Your Subject
    Considering Causes or Effects
    Researching Your Subject
    Analyzing Your Readers
        Learning More about Your Readers: A Collaborative Activity
    Rehearsing Your Argument
Drafting
    Setting Goals
    Planning Your Draft
    Avoiding Logical Fallacies
Reading a Draft Critically
    Reading for a First Impression
    Reading to Analyze
        Presenting the Subject
        Making a Cause or Effect Argument
        Handling Objections and Alternative Causes or Effects
        Establishing Credibility
Revising
    Revising to Improve the Presentation of Your Subject
    Revising to Strengthen Your Cause or Effect Argument
    Revising to Improve Your Handling of Objections and Alternative Causes or Effects
    Revising to Enhance Your Credibility
    Reflecting on What You Have Learned about Writing Essays Speculating about Causes or Effects

Students often complain of difficulty finding a topic, so the text lists some areas where they can look. You might help them by adding some local examples to the list of possibilities.

Some students have trouble understanding the terms *trend* and *phenomenon*. Perhaps the simplest way to define and distinguish these terms would be to say that a trend is a changing pattern of human behavior, while a phenomenon is a pattern that remains constant. Perennial traditions and persistent problems are phenomena; shifts in the pattern of human behavior, and problems that are improving or deteriorating, are trends. If your students find this distinction too subtle, illustrate it by discussing with them the difference between the causes of a longstanding local problem and the causes of a sudden worsening of this problem. Different reasons are needed to explain the changing situation.

Some students also have difficulty distinguishing between a trend and a fad. A trend has some momentum and staying power, and reflects significant changes in behavior or circumstances. Fads may be widespread, but they tend to be short-lived and whimsical—changes in fashion, for instance, caused simply by the human desire for novelty.

When students reach the stage of considering causes or effects, they may need some guidance to distinguish causes from effects, and to distinguish various kinds of causes and effects from each other. Background causes precede and prepare indirectly for an event or a trend; immediate causes trigger it; and perpetuating causes sustain a trend or phenomenon. If they are writing an analysis of effects, students should consider immediate, long-term, and indirect effects of their event, trend, or phenomenon. If it has been around for some time, they may also be able to consider past effects. Ask students to work out the relationships among their causes or effects. For instance, are any of the causes connected? Are there chains of causes to be traced? Which are the most influential causes?

It might be a good idea to assign the invention process up to this point as homework. Then have students discuss their notes in class with you and other students before proceeding with their topics.

Students used to writing only for teachers often have difficulty understanding the importance of analyzing their readers. To help them imagine an audience for their essay, ask them to choose a place where their speculation about causes or effects might be published, and then to describe the readers of this publication. It will also help if they keep a particular reader of this publication—especially a skeptical reader—in mind as they write.

The suggestions given at the goal-setting and planning stages of the composing process make numerous references to the selections in this chapter, reminding students that there are many possible approaches to a speculation about causes or effects. The list of questions points out the kinds of decisions writers often make at this stage in the composing process, just before they begin drafting.

SPECIAL PROBLEMS OF THIS WRITING ASSIGNMENT. One problem with this assignment is that some students who choose to write about a trend are reluctant to demonstrate that a trend is actually a trend, that it is *increasing* or *decreasing* over a specific time period. This task really requires a double argument: the writer must first argue that a trend exists and then argue for some possible causes of it. You will need to give those students who have chosen to write about trends special encouragement and help with this first argument—demonstrating the existence of the trend.

Other problems students may encounter with this task include:

- Choosing a widely recognized trend or phenomenon and presenting only predictable or obvious causes for it so that the reader thinks "So what?"
- Choosing a trend that has very recently changed directions or lost momentum (such as the divorce rate) and thus may be difficult to interpret or project
- Devoting considerable attention to establishing the existence of the phenomenon or trend and neglecting to mention any causes for it
- Failing to consider alternative causes
- Mentioning alternative causes but not refuting or accepting them
- Failing to consider readers' possible objections to proposed causes

Though this writing task is problematic, with your help nearly all students can succeed at it and experience the very great satisfaction of accomplishing an intellectual challenge. The guide to writing has been devised to forestall the problems we mention in this section. Students who use it with care can succeed at this task—if they have your guidance and encouragement.

Responding to the challenge of this assignment, instructors of UCSD's Third College Writing Program some years ago devised a "communal" assignment to orient students to the research and writing possibilities of causal analysis. In the communal assignment, which prepares students for their individual causal essays, small groups (three to five students) work together to research and draft quickly one causal argument, each group developing a different topic.

PROMISING AND UNPROMISING TOPICS. Limit students to topics that must be argued. Steer them away from events with a single, obvious explanation, for which presenting the causes would involve only reporting, not arguing.

Students need careful guidance in choosing topics for this assignment. If they write about phenomena or trends, they should be able to demonstrate that their subjects are phenomena, involving patterns of behavior rather than one-time events, or that they are trends, involving long-term changes in patterns of behavior rather than short-term, faddish shifts.

Some types of topics pose particular challenges for students:

- Historical phenomena or historically completed trends (for instance, an explanation of the increase in brain size during early human evolution). These subjects involve students in a different kind of research than that required by more current topics. These essays tend to read like research reports of others' observations on the subject.
- Phenomena observed in personal life (competitiveness, procrastination, popularity, laziness). Students writing about these topics may tend to rely exclusively on anecdotal information drawn from their own experience, rather than generalizing from their own experience to much larger conclusions about the phenomenon.
- Trends relating to technology (increased use of videocassette recorders, declining cost of handheld calculators, increasing use of personal stereos). Students often choose to write about these subjects because it is easy to document the existence of the trend itself; however, students have difficulty in going beyond the obvious explanation of technological advances in analyzing the causes of the trends.

- Subjects that could be approached as either phenomena or trends (teenage suicide, popular activities like windsurfing or snowboarding). Students will need to decide whether to treat the topic as a trend or as a phenomenon.

Since topic choice is a special problem, you might try this activity. After discussing the readings, list several possible events, phenomena, or trend topics on the board. Ask students in groups of two or three to choose a topic and prepare a defense of it for the class. They must argue that the topic is actually an event, a phenomenon, or a trend (and not a fad), that it is a researchable essay topic, that its causes are not already settled and therefore still require speculation, and that the topic will interest some particular readers they identify.

You will no doubt think of additional ways to enable students to propose and evaluate topics.

Chapter 8 PROPOSAL TO SOLVE A PROBLEM

Although simple in structure, proposals are one of the most complex kinds of argument because they can incorporate so many other kinds of writing—most, in fact, of the kinds presented in the preceding chapters of this book. Writers often begin a proposal with personal experience of a problem, for example, or by reflecting on a problem they have observed but not experienced. If readers are unfamiliar with the problem, it must be explained in enough detail to convince them that it exists. Writers also need to evaluate the problem, to demonstrate that it is a problem; the most common way to do this is by describing its negative effects, present and future. Since the best solutions treat a problem at its root, analyzing the causes of the problem can provide the criteria necessary to evaluate possible solutions. Writers can also evaluate solutions by conjecturing regarding their likely effects. Proposals, then, usually involve a combination of other kinds of writing, some of it argumentative, some of it merely informative, and they draw on a wide range of writing skills. They are an important and common kind of writing in most fields, and many students can expect to write proposals at some point during their post-college careers.

You might survey the many contexts in which proposals are typically written. Although students do not ordinarily read such proposal writing in school, public policy and business could not function without proposals. Studying proposal writing helps students learn to reconceive situations in terms of problems and solutions. The educational system teaches students to think in terms of good and bad (appropriate to writing evaluations), cause and effect (appropriate to speculation about causes and effects), and right and wrong (appropriate to position papers), but not in terms of problem and solution (appropriate to proposals). Nevertheless, problem-solving is basic to creativity and an invaluable way of looking at the world.

WRITING ASSIGNMENT: Proposal to Solve a Problem
This is the writing assignment that appears near the beginning of Chapter 8:

Write an essay, proposing a solution to a clearly defined problem affecting a group or community to which you belong. Your task is to establish that the problem exists, to offer a solution that can reasonably be implemented, to lay out the particulars by which your proposal would be put into effect, and to consider objections and alternative solutions.

Possible subjects students might write about (Considering Ideas for Your Own Writing) follow each reading, and additional suggestions appear in the Invention section of the Guide to Writing Proposals to Solve a Problem.

Writing Situations for Proposing Solutions to Problems

The chapter opens with four writing situations that suggest a range of occasions when proposals might be written. One of the situations involves writing for a college political science course, while another is written for an economics course. There is one business writing situation, certainly one of the most common areas for proposal writing. The situation on AIDS tracing deals with a menacing social problem.

You could give a brief presentation to your students on the rhetorical features of one of the situations. Using your presentation as a model, students could then work in small groups to develop their own presentations on the rhetorical features of the remaining situations, each small group taking one situation. After all the groups have given their presentations to the class, discussion could center on the similarities and differences among the rhetorical features of the situations. Here is our rhetorical analysis of the third situation, the proposal written in a political science class:

Topic: the four-year presidency
Writer: college student
Audience: the professor, hypothetical policymakers
Problem: presidents are only productive for half of their four-year terms
Reason: they spend too much time getting organized, running for reelection, or being lame ducks
Evidence: examples from recent history
Solution: a six-year nonrenewable presidential term
Reason: it would give presidents four or five years of good time
Objections: it could make presidents less responsive to the public will
Refutation: the system of legislative checks and balances would prevent this problem
Alternative solution: none

Practicing Proposing Solutions to Problems: A Collaborative Activity

Conducting this group activity so early in the process, long before they begin to consider their own topics and even before they discuss the chapter readings, students will nevertheless be drawn surprisingly quickly into the complexities and possibilities of proposing solutions to problems. This activity has the benefits of preparing the students for the readings and anticipating the entire chapter. After about fifteen minutes, shift the students to Part 2 of the activity, which asks them to step back and reflect together on the experience. After a few more minutes, shift the focus to whole-class discussion to share reflections on and reactions to the process of proposing solutions.

A GUIDE TO READING A PROPOSAL TO SOLVE A PROBLEM

This section reminds students that they will be reading the selections in this chapter both as readers and as writers of proposals to solve problems. For class activities to use in conjunction with this section, see Part 5 of this manual.

Here, following a brief illustration of annotation, we present a sample essay by Robert Samuelson. As you preview the essay for your students, you might ask them to consider how Samuelson's audience—*Newsweek* readers—affects his presentation of both the problem he introduces and the solution he proposes.

Reading for Meaning

This section, like corresponding sections following each reading selection in the chapter, encourages students to explore their understanding of Samuelson's proposal. The section gives students a range of specific suggestions for initiating and sustaining their explorations of Samuelson's argument; students are also asked to consider his purpose and audience, and to relate their own observations and experiences to Samuelson's assertions.

Reading like a Writer

In this section, students are encouraged to shift their focus from the content of the essay to the specific strategies used by the writer to achieve his purpose. Strategies employed by writers of proposals to solve problems include *introducing the problem, presenting the solution,* and *convincing readers to accept the solution.* In the critical reading and writing tasks that follow, each of these strategies is broken down more specifically: *introducing the problem* requires that writers both describe the problem and declare its significance, while *presenting the solution* requires writers to describe the solution and to show readers how the solution could be implemented. *Convincing readers to accept the solution* is discussed in terms of arguing directly for the solution and counterarguing readers' objections and questions, and evaluating alternative solutions.

The Reading like a Writer section following the sample essay presents a full range of strategies for writing proposals. Corresponding sections following each of the subsequent reading selections in the chapter will focus more closely on one or two strategies particularly appropriate to the analysis of each essay.

Introducing the Problem. Because Samuelson's proposed solution rests, in part, on his belief that the problem has not been recognized or adequately identified, this strategy is especially central to the success of his argument. Where other observers attribute the weakness of our educational system to schools or to teachers, Samuelson locates the problem in the students themselves. Students—many of them recently out of high school—will readily see that, in so doing, Samuelson runs the risk of alienating a substantial part of his audience. Students will probably suggest that Samuelson might have strengthened this aspect of his argument by providing more and different types of information in support of his interpretation of the problem.

Writers of proposals must also convince their readers of the significance of the problems they present. Especially if your students have completed the speculation about causes or effects presented in Chapter 7 of the text, they should have no problem recognizing that the analysis of both the causes and, especially, the effects of lack of motivation among students plays a major role in Samuelson's argument for the significance and pervasiveness of the problem. Again, you can expect students to remain somewhat critical of Samuelson's seeming inability or unwillingness to defend his redefinition of what he clearly considers a serious problem.

Presenting the Solution. Many students will find Samuelson's actual presentation of his proposed solution rather sketchy. Although this section mentions the tentative and speculative nature of Samuelson's solution, you might want to remind students of this before they respond to the task.

Likewise, this might be a good opportunity to remind students of the centrality of purpose and audience in our consideration of each essay, and of the roles these play in this particular essay. As they evaluate Samuelson's decision not to detail the implementation of his proposed solution, students will want to consider how Samuelson expects his readers to react to his argument. Most students are likely to agree with the evaluation implied in the writing task in this section: that Samuelson might easily have done more to suggest how his solution might be implemented.

Convincing Readers to Accept the Solution. Here we draw students' attention to the strategies of direct argument for a solution, counterargument, and evaluating alternative solutions. Students should have little trouble recognizing Samuelson's direct argument for his solution, but they may need some help in identifying and analyzing his use of the other two strategies.

This section reminds students of three ways in which writers counterargue readers' objections or questions: by acknowledging, accommodating, or refuting them. Students will encounter these again in the upcoming chapter on writing position papers. In Samuelson's case, students will probably observe that, rather than accommodating possible objections to his position, he refutes them quite bluntly ("Forget it," paragraph 7; "let's be candid," paragraph 14).

In the same way—and much the same tone—in which he refutes possible objections to his position, Samuelson unequivocally rejects the alternate solutions suggested in paragraphs 10 and 11, dismissing them as "fictitious," "irrelevant," and failures. Students will probably note that Samuelson's use of this strategy fits in with the overall pattern and tone of his argument.

In the paragraphs specified at the end of this task, Samuelson argues for his solution primarily by presenting his personal opinions, backed up in several places by statistical evidence. Students may suggest that a wider range of types of evidence might have helped Samuelson argue for his solution more convincingly. Some students may be especially troubled by the elusiveness of Samuelson's argument for his solution, pointing out that the evidence in the paragraphs in question tends to relate more to the *need* for a solution than to the solution itself.

RESOURCES FOR TEACHING THE READINGS

The readings in this chapter address a range of education, social, political, and work-related problems. The first essay, by Mark Kleiman, proposes an alternative way of getting a B.A. degree. Next comes Edward J. Loughran's proposal for preventing juvenile delinquency.

John Beilenson proposes giving young volunteers a larger voice in national service programs, while Toby Haynsworth and Gerald Perselay propose an ambitious apprenticeship program for American high school students. The final essay, written by Will Scarvie, a student, illustrates proposal writing in the workplace.

Students can learn from these essays that proposals are written in a variety of different tones and styles, and that they share common features: they must define the problem clearly, demonstrate that it exists and that it has harmful consequences, and support the solution by arguing that it would be effective, feasible, and better than the alternatives. Students can also learn from the readings that proposal writers must gauge how much readers know about the problem and what difficulty they might have accepting the proposed solution, and that they must find ways of overcoming readers' resistance.

The following material introduces each reading and explores the possibilities offered by the sections on reading for meaning and reading like a writer and the ideas for writing that follow each reading.

Mark Kleiman, **Confer College Degrees by Examination**

To college students, this article should be a provocative introduction to proposals. There should be no difficulty in generating discussion, but you might help students preview the article by asking what they think the purpose of a college education is and what they think a degree is presently worth in the marketplace. The headnote gives a brief overview of the essay and asks students to consider why getting a college degree might be viewed as problematic. Because Kleiman's proposal is controversial, students should be encouraged to respond to his argument, pointing out shortcomings he has failed to mention or alternatives he has overlooked.

Reading for Meaning

This section asks students to consider how Kleiman's purpose and audience affect his approach to his argument. Students are also invited to explore their understanding of the problem Kleiman locates, and of the solution he proposes. In addition, they are encouraged to consider Kleiman's argument in light of their own educational experience. As usual after the first reading selection in each chapter, we suggest that you collect students' writing for this activity, reading over it quickly to see how they're doing and perhaps reading a few responses out loud in class.

Extending Meaning through Conversation. Students can continue to develop their understanding of the meaning of Kleiman's essay by talking about it with one or two classmates. You might help students get started on this activity by once again reminding them of Kleiman's projected audience—business managers. Invite students to imagine themselves in this position, and ask each to comment on how he or she would receive Kleiman's proposal. If students find they respond differently, which they undoubtedly will, this will be a useful basis for further discussion of the proposal, both in their small groups and in the class as a whole.

Reading like a Writer: Convincing Readers to Accept the Solution by Counterarguing Objections

Kleiman considers two objections to his proposed solution. He acknowledges the possible truth of the first—that people who get degrees by exam "might miss out on the opportunities college provides for social interaction and other forms of personal and intellectual development"—but suggests that it is "not conclusive." Some students may feel that, as Kleiman's audience is less likely to be concerned with "social interaction" than with the financial bottom line, it is perhaps natural for Kleiman to brush this objection aside. Kleiman responds to the second objection—that "B.A.'s by exam" would be denied the breadth and depth of a standard college education—in somewhat more detail, by modifying and expanding on his solution. Students are also encouraged to suggest objections in addition to the two mentioned by Kleiman; most will have no trouble coming up with one or more fairly serious objections to his argument.

We suggest that you approach the Analyze section of this activity as a group before students write up their individual responses. You would lead students through the text, showing them how to do a thorough analysis by rereading, annotating, and taking notes. Once students have completed the Write portion of the activity, be sure to have some students share their responses in class, both so that you can monitor how well they are understanding the material and as a starting point for further class discussion.

Considering Ideas for Your Own Writing

While we often discourage students from taking on problems at the state or national level unless we are sure they will have adequate time to do research, we find that many students are successful at writing proposals to solve problems they have observed or experienced on their own campuses. These topics are accessible to students, and they enjoy writing about issues that relate to their everyday lives.

Edward J. Loughran, **Prevention of Delinquency**

Loughran's essay offers an expert's point of view on a disturbing trend: the increasing number of young people who are put in jail each year. In the introductory note to the section, students are encouraged to consider the trend itself before reading the essay, and to note the way Loughran presents the problem.

Reading for Meaning

To explore and clarify their understanding of Loughran's arguments, students are asked to paraphrase Loughran's solution and then to examine his argument. As usual, we offer a number of further suggestions for making meaning from the text, ending with the suggestion that students can make meaning from the essay by analyzing their own experiences and observations in light of Loughran's presentation of both the problem and the solution.

Extending Meaning through Conversation. As students develop their understanding of the meaning of the essay by discussing it with one or two classmates, you might want to circulate among pairs or groups, helping students keep personal experience or opinion tied explicitly to the text. If you find that students have strong feelings about this topic, you could ask one member of each pair or group to share the results of this activity in class as a way of generating useful discussion of Loughran's argument.

Judging the Writer's Credibility (A Further Strategy for Reading for Meaning). Before students begin this activity, have them see the section on judging a writer's credibility in Appendix 1, A Catalog of Critical Reading Strategies, where they will find a demonstration of the strategy in use. Periodically throughout this textbook, we refer students to supplemental activities outlined in the appendices to the text, each of which is designed to help students further develop their understanding of the particular genre. Once students have completed this activity, you might have them share their written responses, either in small groups or as part of a larger class discussion. While most students will find Loughran's argument credible, it is important that they also understand *why* it is credible.

Reading like a Writer: Introducing the Problem

Alerted by the introductory material preceding the selection, students will probably have noticed that Loughran goes into considerably more detail in presenting the problem than do the writers of the two previous essays. If your students have recently completed the assignment in writing about causes or effects in Chapter 7, they will probably recognize Loughran's strategy in presenting the problem: as is the case for many writers analyzing the causes of a trend, if Loughran can show that the trend in question exists, most readers will accept without question the significance of the trend. Thus, Loughran relies on statistics to demonstrate the existence of the problem, and on a brief causal analysis (paragraphs 8–11) to lead from his discussion of the problem to his presentation of a solution.

Considering Ideas for Your Own Writing

This section gives students a range of fairly specific suggestions for writing about social problems. Once again, we steer students away from overly broad topics, encouraging them to focus on "immediate, local, troublesome social problems." Since the best proposals tend to be ones in which the writer has some personal involvement or to be based on problems the writer can observe closely, it is advisable to restrict students' choices to some degree.

John Beilenson, **Giving the Young a Voice in National Service Programs**

Beilenson identifies a problem in what he otherwise sees as a good program: the absence or paucity of "youth voice" in President Clinton's National Service Corporation. Students should note that Beilenson's proposed solution is broken down into several components, and that, in addition to his proposal, he outlines its effects and benefits in some detail.

Reading for Meaning

Here, as we often do in this section, we ask students to begin exploring the meaning of the text by summarizing a key passage. You might take this opportunity to remind students of the importance of summarizing and paraphrasing as critical reading strategies. We give students a number of other suggestions for making meaning from the text individually before they proceed to the following activity.

Extending Meaning through Conversation. As students continue to develop their understanding of Beilenson's argument by discussing it with one or two classmates, we ask them to begin by considering Beilenson's audience. Remind students that proposal essays are usually meant to elicit action on the parts of their audience; ask them to speculate about how successful Beilenson's proposal is likely to be, given what they know about his readers. As students proceed with their conversation about this piece, they may find that some of them detect a slight "us-them" tone—a rather artificial distinction between "young people" and "adults"—while others may find Beilenson's presentation of this distinction perfectly acceptable. We encourage students to explore these differences in understanding as they discuss the essay.

Reading like a Writer: Presenting the Solution

The introductory material for this task reminds students once again that the writer's awareness of his audience helps to determine the overall shape of his argument—in Beilenson's case, leading him to present his solution, as does Loughran, in more detail than do Kleiman and Samuelson. We steer students back to the six paragraphs where Beilenson presents his solution; as students reread and annotate this section of the essay, they should see that, in addition to breaking his solution down into five clear components, Beilenson also anticipates readers' questions or objections, stating, for instance, that "the over-30 crowd . . . need not worry" in paragraph 5. Once students have completed the writing portion of this activity, you might ask a few of them to share their responses in class, both as a way of monitoring how well they are understanding the material and of encouraging discussion of the essay.

Considering Ideas for Your Own Writing

These ideas offer specific guidelines and suggestions for thinking about problems related to organizations or institutions. Most students will readily be able to come up with one or two examples of such problems. If you wanted to use this as a class activity, you could have the whole class brainstorm to generate a list of problems, help them narrow it down to the two or three most interesting issues, and ask them to speculate as a group on how they might research and present solutions to these problems.

Toby Haynsworth and Gerald Perselay, **A U.S. Youth Apprenticeship Program**

Students will by now have noticed that each of the proposals in the chapter so far, including the sample essay by Robert J. Samuelson, deals with a topic affecting young people; in the case of this essay, the authors propose the adoption of a broad-based youth apprenticeship program in order to mitigate what they see to be weaknesses in the U.S. educational system. Students will want to pay specific attention to the authors' handling of alternate solutions; this may be an important consideration in their own proposal essays.

Reading for Meaning

As always, this section asks students to scrutinize the content of the essay closely, relating it to their own experience where appropriate. If you find that students are using their personal experience to make meaning from the text, you might invite them to do so orally in class, making sure that they do not move entirely away from the essay itself, but that they continue to make explicit connections between their experiences and the text.

Extending Meaning through Conversation. We ask students to begin their small-group discussion by considering Haynsworth and Perselay's audience. Remind students that they will need to continue rereading and annotating the essay as they develop their understanding of its meaning through conversation. Once again, especially if you find that students are relying heavily on their own experience to make meaning from the text, you might want to circulate among groups, making sure conversations are remaining anchored in the text itself.

Reading like a Writer: Convincing Readers to Accept the Solution by Evaluating Alternate Solutions

Here, we help students begin to appreciate the important role of alternate solutions in proposal essays. Students who have not been exposed to this type of writing before may assume that introducing alternate—often competing—solutions might weaken an argument; with this essay, we help them see that alternate solutions must be taken into account, and that, as writers either dismiss them or incorporate them into their own proposed solutions, alternate solutions actually strengthen this type of argument. Once students have completed the writing portion of this activity, you might have them share their responses, either in small groups or as a class as a way of facilitating discussion of the essay.

Considering Ideas for Your Own Writing

In this section, we continue the theme of alternate or competing solutions, asking students to imagine themselves in the position of proposing a solution that is different from the favored or obvious solution. As students begin to consider topics for their own essays, we generally encourage them to address subjects with which they have had experience or which they've been able to observe; in this case, we invite them to consider writing a proposal essay about a school- or campus-wide program. You might have each student come up with one or two ideas, and then share them in class.

Will Scarvie, **Proposal to Increase Efficiency in the Computer Section**

While many students may not find the content of Scarvie's proposal engaging, how he responds to the situation in which he is writing should interest them. This selection may encourage some of your students to write proposals that they could submit in their workplaces, communities, or schools.

Reading for Meaning

Because Scarvie's proposal is presented as a memo to his superior, considerations of audience and purpose may seem especially immediate to students. Most students will recognize that, because Scarvie's audience is defined as it is, he must be especially diplomatic, taking extreme care to avoid appearing either ill-informed about or overly critical of the existing situation. Since students know from the introductory note to the selection that Scarvie's proposal was in fact implemented, students will want to focus on *why* it was taken seriously.

Extending Meaning through Conversation. As students develop their understanding of the meaning of Scarvie's essay through conversation, they will need to continue to reread and annotate, keeping the basic features of proposal writing in mind as they comment on the strengths and weaknesses of the essay.

Reading like a Writer: Convincing Readers to Accept the Solution

If students make a scratch outline of Scarvie's proposal as they annotate, they will see that it follows a logical order: Scarvie begins by introducing the problem—the backlog of projects in the computer section—and then proceeds to identify the cause of the problem. As in Loughran's essay earlier in the chapter, Scarvie uses a brief causal analysis to lead from his discussion of the problem into his proposed solution. The solution is presented in two parts: a comprehensive planning chart and a coordinator for the computer section. Scarvie goes on to introduce and dismiss an alternate solution, and then to anticipate three objections his reader might raise. He refutes the charge that his solution would be "cumbersome," although he acknowledges that some time and expense would be involved in hiring a coordinator. He also acknowledges that it will be difficult to estimate how much time projects will take, but suggests that this difficulty will lessen once the plan is implemented.

Most students will find Scarvie's organization solid and effective. A few may suggest that, in addition to identifying the *cause* of the problem, Scarvie might have gone into the *effects* of the problem as well, thus strengthening the reader's impression of its significance.

Reading like a Writer: A Follow-up Activity

Once students have completed the last Reading like a Writer activity, they will have generated quite a bit of written commentary about the readings in the chapter. You can help them review what they have learned by having them look back over the writing they have done, choosing one piece to revise and expand through further analysis. They would then turn in this revised writing with their final essay packages or in their end-of-course portfolios.

Considering Ideas for Your Own Writing

This section urges students to think of problems related to their own jobs. We find that students do best writing proposals for work sites or organizations with which they are familiar. Students are invited to practice describing the problem, proposing a solution, and searching for alternate solutions.

THINKING ABOUT WHAT MAKES PROPOSALS EFFECTIVE

As we do following the reading selections in each chapter of this text, we ask students to review and consolidate what they have learned about writing in each genre. Referring students back to the list of features of successful proposals—originally presented following the sample essay by Robert J. Samuelson early in the chapter—we invite students to choose the one essay from the chapter they believe to be the most successful in achieving its purpose and fulfilling these features. Asking students to justify their choices helps them focus even more closely on the features of the genre.

A GUIDE TO WRITING PROPOSALS TO SOLVE PROBLEMS

The guide leads students through a composing process that follows these steps:

Invention
    Choosing a Problem
    Analyzing the Problem and Identifying a Solution
    Considering Your Readers
        Learning More about Your Readers: A Collaborative Activity
    Developing an Argument
    Researching Your Proposal
Drafting
    Setting Goals
    Planning Your Draft
    Beginning
    Avoiding Logical Fallacies

Proposal writing is ideal for helping students develop audience awareness—necessary for all writing, but essential for persuasion. You might have students work in small groups and take turns playing the role of their classmates' intended readers. After describing his or her intended reader, the writer could summarize the problem and then briefly argue for the proposed solution. The group would then respond as the intended reader might. Since each group member would be likely to respond somewhat differently, a discussion about audience is likely to ensue.

In setting goals, students should reconsider their purpose and readers and adopt a tone suitable to both. Although the text describes a general organization they might follow and suggests ways they might begin their essays, remind students that writers have many options and that their decisions must be made in the context of their particular purpose and audience.

To alert students to common pitfalls in reasoning, the text lists some logical fallacies typical of proposal writing. Students should keep those fallacies in mind as they draft and certainly refer to them when they revise. The either/or and the "straw man" fallacies are generally the most troubling to students.

Again, remind students to keep their purpose and audience in focus as they revise. In particular, stress the importance of building their argument upon a solid foundation of shared values and beliefs. You might invite them to explore these underlying assumptions in writing before revising their essays.

SPECIAL PROBLEMS OF THIS WRITING ASSIGNMENT. Special difficulties students sometimes encounter as they write proposals involve topic choice and the need to establish the problem's existence and seriousness. Even though students are asked to write about a problem faced by a group to which they belong, they sometimes take on problems that are too abstract or complicated for them to handle effectively in a short time. It is understandable that students should want to solve some of the major problems we as a society face—such as the threat of nuclear annihilation, the lack of shelter for the homeless, or the deterioration of our industrial urban centers. As much as we do not want to discourage students from trying to understand these problems and even possibly contributing to their solutions, we also do not want them to fail in their attempts to write successful proposals because their writing is too general. This chapter is designed to teach students how to gather the information they need to make their writing more specific.

A good proposal does two things: it defines a problem and then argues for a particular solution. We have found that even the student who argues effectively for a solution may sometimes fail to establish the problem's existence and seriousness. Defining the problem actually requires careful assessment of the rhetorical situation. The student must decide just how aware of the problem the readers are and how best to convince them that it is worthy of their attention and possibly their time and money as well.

PROMISING AND UNPROMISING TOPICS. Choosing an appropriate topic is probably the hardest part of proposal writing. Some students know immediately what they want to write about, while others are at a loss. Perhaps the greatest stumbling block is abstractness. The more distant the problem is from the writer's personal experience the harder it is to write about. That is why we urge students to choose a problem plaguing a community or group to which they belong. Even the most abstract problems can be treated in the context of a local group. Those concerned with broad educational problems, for example, might find evidence of the problem in their own high school or college. Those concerned with social and economic problems like homelessness and unemployment might look in their communities.

Writing about a problem in a group to which they belong will also help students with the crucial task of analyzing their readers. They can more easily anticipate possible objections to their solution and alternative solutions others might offer. They can also draw on common values and experience to establish the seriousness of the problem and argue for the feasibility of the proposed solution.

Chapter 9 POSITION PAPER

The introduction to this chapter contrasts the position paper with the proposal, pointing out that proposals have a specific, practical purpose, whereas position papers tend to be more general and philosophical. The position paper relates to the proposal in rather the same way that the reflective essay relates to the autobiographical essay. Just as reflective writing differs from autobiographical writing in its "fierce attachment to an idea," so the position paper differs from the proposal in its central concern for principles. The crux of a proposal is often a pragmatic issue—whether a particular solution will solve the problem at hand; at the heart of a position paper there are nearly always ethical questions, values, and assumptions—questions of right and wrong that can seldom be resolved by facts alone.

When students take a position on a controversial issue, they discover not only that people differ but also that they have good reasons for their different views. They learn to respect the complexity of these issues and the subtlety of others' reasoning. Because these chapters emphasize the rhetorical aspects of argumentation, they help students avoid polemics. Students learn to develop an argument that is responsive to their readers' concerns, that builds a bridge of shared values.

The writing assignment requires that students examine the issue critically. Instead of framing an argument to support an already-formed opinion, we encourage students to analyze and evaluate the pros and cons of the issue before reaching their own conclusions. We urge them to examine their own underlying assumptions as critically as they would those of their opponents. We want them to recognize the value of thinking through the issue and of basing their position on solid reasoning and evidence, not merely to convince others but for their own sake as well.

WRITING ASSIGNMENT: Arguing a Position on an Issue

Here is the writing assignment that appears near the beginning of Chapter 9:

> Write an essay that argues a position on a controversial issue. Take into account readers' objections, questions, and opposing viewpoints, but remember that your purpose is to state your own position clearly and to convince those who disagree with you that they must take seriously the arguments you raise.

Possible issues students might write about (Considering Ideas for Your Own Writing) follow each reading selection. In addition, suggestions appear in the Invention section of the Guide to Writing Position Papers.

Writing Situations for Arguing Positions on Issues

The three brief writing situations presented early in the chapter demonstrate that writers argue for positions on controversial issues in both academic and nonacademic settings. The situations also suggest some of the many issues debated in position papers: the regulation of urban development, surrogate motherhood, and the right of public employees to strike. You might ask your students to brainstorm a list of other issues even before reading further in the chapter, or you might refer back to these writing situations just before asking students to list topics on which they might consider writing.

Practicing Arguing a Position: A Collaborative Activity

As the introductory paragraph suggests, this activity will reassure students that they already know a great deal about arguing a position; it will also alert them to certain challenges of this type of writing that they may not have anticipated. As usual, this is a two-part activity; students are asked first to debate an issue with a partner, and then to reflect on the argument process itself. Although this activity may seem time-consuming, it is a very effective method of orienting students to the upcoming writing task.

A GUIDE TO READING POSITION PAPERS

This section leads students through the critical reading and writing strategies they will use throughout the chapter. For class activities to be used in conjunction with this section, see Part 5 of this manual.

The sample essay provided in this section, following a brief illustration of annotation, clearly demonstrates the central features of writing to take a position: defining the issue, asserting a clear and unequivocal position, arguing directly for a position, and counterarguing objections and opposing positions. The Reading like a Writer section following the essay will break these down into more specific strategies.

Dick Teresi's essay, which argues that helmet laws should be repealed, provides a useful bridge from the proposal assignment in the previous chapter to the position paper assignment; students will have little problem seeing the connections between these two types of argument.

Erdrich's example is also useful in that it clearly refers to personal experience as well as drawing on factual information.

Reading for Meaning

This section invites students to respond to the content of the selection, exploring their understanding of and response to Teresi's essay. The section begins by asking students to articulate their own positions on the issue of helmet laws; it then encourages them to respond to his argument, which students will find more or less convincing depending on their own experience and observations. You might give students five or ten minutes of class time to write about their responses to the suggestions in this section, and then use those responses as the starting point for class discussion of the essay.

Reading like a Writer

This section helps students move from examining the content and purpose of the essay to analyzing the features of this type of writing and the specific strategies used by the writer to accomplish her purpose. The tasks in this section directly anticipate the thinking students will do as they read the other selections in this chapter and as they begin to work on their own essays. The section introduces students to the major elements of writing to take a position: *defining the issue, asserting a clear and unequivocal position, arguing directly for a position, and counterarguing objections and opposing positions.* Students will probably recognize that defining the issue and indicating its significance are strategies parallel to ones in earlier assignment chapters; this section will also remind them that the writer must assert a clear, unequivocal position and also acknowledge the opposing position. Students will see that convincing readers to take the position seriously requires that the writer argue directly for the position and counterargue against readers' objections and questions.

The Reading like a Writer section following the sample essay presents a full range of strategies for writing to take a position. Corresponding sections following each of the reading selections in the chapter will focus more narrowly on strategies particularly appropriate to the analysis of each essay. You may want to remind students once again that they are responsible for responding thoughtfully and specifically to the activities in these sections.

Defining the Issue. This exercise directs students' attention to the fact that writers of position papers must inform their readers about the issue as well as convincing them of its significance. Because Teresi can assume that most readers are familiar with helmet laws, he needn't spend much time presenting the issue itself; instead, he can proceed to define the issue in his own terms. Where many opponents of helmet laws see such laws as a threat to individual liberty, Teresi clearly frames the issue as one of safety, arguing that these laws, in fact, do not protect motorcycle riders from injury.

Asserting a Clear, Unequivocal Position. This section reminds students that, while informing readers about the issue is certainly part of a writer's task in taking a position, writers must go beyond the mere reporting of information and assert a definitive position on the issue. In pointing out that writers may choose to assert their positions at different points in their essays, this section foreshadows the upcoming discussion of devising a logical plan.

In the case of Teresi's essay, students are asked to pinpoint his assertion wherever this assertion appears in his essay. Possibly drawing on their responses to previous exercises, students should be able to report that Teresi's position, or "thesis," is stated relatively late in his essay, toward the end of the third paragraph ("we oppose the laws . . ."). They should also note that his thesis is arguable: in stating a position that flies in the face of what many readers believe about motorcycle safety, he seems openly to invite opposing viewpoints.

Arguing Directly for the Position. The introduction to this section directs students' attention to the kind of reasoning writers of position papers use; we also invite them to consider how the awareness of their audiences affects writers' approaches to position papers. Students are asked to comment specifically in writing on Teresi's reasons for his position. Students will note that he relies on a combination of different types of information, ranging from what is undoubtedly personal experience to the use of statistics, in support of his position. You could use this as a class activity, asking students to identify specific reasons and keeping a list of these on the board, as a way of helping students understand this feature.

Counterarguing Objections and Opposing Positions. This section reminds students that writers of position papers must anticipate readers' objections and opposing positions; most students will have little trouble noting that Teresi confronts objections head-on, using rhetorical questions, for instance, at the beginnings of paragraphs 5 and 7 to introduce—and quickly refute—possible opposing arguments. Students will probably vary in how convincing they find Teresi's counterarguments: while some will be satisfied that he has proved his point, others may find his attitude somewhat cavalier.

RESOURCES FOR TEACHING THE READINGS

The readings in this chapter take up a variety of controversial issues. The sample essay by Dick Teresi concerns the safety issues surrounding motorcycle helmet laws. The second selection, by Stephen Bates, focuses on important issues of religious tolerance, while Donella Meadows takes a position against media talk shows. Next comes Charles Krauthammer's argument against "sentimental environmentalism," and Shelby Steele's argument regarding the role of affirmative action programs. The final selection on sex education in schools was written by Jill Kuhn, a student.

The following material discusses each reading and offers advice on using the sections on reading for meaning and reading like a writer and the ideas for writing that follow each reading.

Stephen Bates, **Religious Diversity and the Schools**

Bates's essay addresses the timely and controversial issue of separation of church and state, in the form of religious tolerance in schools. The introductory note asks students to consider what they know about the history of the issue before reading Bates's argument.

Reading for Meaning

Here, students are asked to go back to the text to explore their understanding of the meaning of Bates's argument. As usual, we ask them to begin by paraphrasing the argument, putting Bates's position in their own words in order to clarify their own understanding. Because any topic dealing with religion is likely to elicit highly personal reactions in some readers, you might monitor students' responses to this piece by inviting them to share their writing in class;

in this way, you can not only see how well they are understanding the material, but also make sure that they do not stray too far away from the text itself in making meaning.

Extending Meaning through Conversation. Likewise, you might find it helpful to circulate among groups during this part of the activity, listening for indications that personal experience or beliefs may be drawing conversations too far off track, and offering suggestions to help students make explicit connections between their experience and the text.

Reading like a Writer: Defining the Issue

Students should recall from their work with the sample essay by Dick Teresi that writers of position papers often have some options in defining the issue in question: where Teresi defines the issue of helmet laws as one of safety rather than of individual rights, Bates offers a surprising twist on the issue of religion in the schools by pointing out that a system that purports to promote tolerance is actually *in*tolerant in some ways. We direct students' attention specifically to the paragraphs in which he presents the issue, asking them to make a scratch outline as they reread and annotate; you might take this opportunity to remind students of the value of keeping an informal outline as a critical reading strategy.

For this first reading selection in the chapter, we suggest that you lead the class in the Analyze portion of the activity, perhaps constructing a scratch outline as a group on the board, before having students complete the Write section of the activity on their own.

Considering Ideas for Your Own Writing

Here, we ask students to consider writing their own position papers about issues based on educational policies. Most students will readily come up with one or two possible ideas; you might make this a group activity by having each student come up with a possible topic, listing these on the board, and then discussing them in class.

Donella Meadows, **Rush and Larry, Coast to Coast: This Is Not Democracy in Action**

This essay considers the role of media talk shows in a democracy; as the title suggests, Meadows argues that these shows are not the democratic forums that they are often assumed to be. Most students will be familiar with one or more of the programs Meadows mentions, and we ask them to reflect on their own opinions about these shows before reading Meadows's essay.

Reading for Meaning

In this section, as usual, we encourage students to continue to reread and annotate as they develop their understanding of the text, paraphrasing Meadows's presentation of the issue and going on to explore other specific aspects of the essay before discussing their insights with one or two other students in the following activity.

Extending Meaning through Conversation. Because this essay touches on politics (the right-wing talk-show host Rush Limbaugh, for instancee, is one of Meadows's prime examples), student discussions of the meaning of the essay are likely to be lively and interesting. To ensure that students do not stray too far from the text itself in their conversations, you might circulate among pairs or groups, offering comments that help students make connections between their experience and the essay. You could also allow some class time following this activity so that students can share the meanings resulting from their conversations.

Reading like a Writer: Making a Position Clear and Unequivocal

As students analyze and write briefly about Meadows's argument, they should have little trouble seeing that her position is stated quite clearly at several points in the essay, including paragraphs 4–5, 9, and 10. This exercise will be particularly useful for students who, perhaps based on high school writing experience, are looking for a single, clearly discernible "thesis statement." You might suggest that students once again use the critical reading strategy of making a scratch outline as they read and reread Meadows' essay, noting the passages where her position is stated most strongly.

Compare. Once or twice in each chapter, we ask students to develop their understanding of a writer's use of a particular strategy more fully by comparing it to another writer's use of the same strategy. Here, we ask students to focus on various writers' presentation of their theses; students will probably note that many of the writers in this chapter avoid opening bluntly with a cut-and-dried thesis statement, as many students have been taught to do.

Considering Ideas for Your Own Writing

This section asks students to consider writing an essay about a controversial issue involving the media. Options suggested here revolve around regulation of various media—a rich source of topic possibilities for many students.

Charles Krauthammer, Saving Nature, but Only for Man

While Meadows writes for readers who may very likely sympathize with her position, Krauthammer takes a position that is likely to be unpopular with his audience, including many students. The introductory note asks students to monitor their initial responses to Krauthammer's argument.

Reading for Meaning

Because Krauthammer's position on this issue is somewhat unpopular, students may have quite a lot to say in response to this section. Students should take the time to consider carefully Krauthammer's assumptions regarding his audience; this should help students, as the text suggests, to understand not only the issue itself but Krauthammer's position and their own reactions to his argument.

Extending Meaning through Conversation. As students continue to make meaning from the essay by discussing Krauthammer's argument in pairs or small groups, we remind them to stay focused on the issue as Krauthammer presents it. To help students avoid straying into highly personal reactions to Krauthammer's position, you might remind students to reread and annotate at least parts of the essay together.

Looking for Patterns of Opposition (A Further Strategy for Reading for Meaning). Krauthammer presents some of the terms in which he defines the issue as sets of oppositions—a strategy inexperienced readers may not have noticed. Here, as we do periodically throughout the text, we refer students to Appendix 1: A Catalog of Critical Reading Strategies. You may find that you need to help students see how sets of oppositions

123

such as "sane" vs. "sentimental" or "necessities" vs. "luxuries" help Krauthammer present his position.

Reading like a Writer: Counterarguing

Here, we direct students' attention to the specific paragraphs in which Krauthammer argues against what he labels "sentimental environmentalism," asking them to examine his refutation of this position and to write briefly about it. You might have students share their responses to this activity, either in small groups or in class, as a way of generating discussion of the important strategy of counterarguing.

Compare. As students compare Krauthammer's use of counterargument to that of another author in the chapter, you will want to remind students that writers of position papers have some options in dealing with possible objections or opposing positions: they can refute them, as Krauthammer does here, or they can modify their own positions to accommodate valid objections; in addition, writers have the option of choosing the tone they feel will be the most effective with their particular audiences. Most students will already have noticed the distinctive tone of Krauthammer's argument, which some students are bound to find somewhat abrasive. Encourage them to compare this tone carefully with that of one of the other writers in the chapter.

Considering Ideas for Your Own Writing

This section suggests three different general types of topics students might consider for their own essays. You might help them anticipate the particular challenges and rewards of each type of subject. First, students are asked to consider writing about fairly broad ecological issues such as oil drilling and recycling. While students are likely to have strong feelings on these issues, they will also need to do research to present their subjects and substantiate their positions. Students might also choose to write about environmental issues that are closer to home, perhaps in evidence on campus or in the local community. Students will have learned from the previous proposal assignment that personal interest or even involvement in an issue will very likely strengthen their arguments, but that they will also need to maintain a certain amount of emotional distance from the controversy in question. Last, students are challenged to choose an *unpopular* position, as Krauthammer does.

Shelby Steele, **Affirmative Action**

Like the selection by Charles Krauthammer, Steele's essay seems to take an unpopular, or at least surprising, position in objecting to affirmative action programs as they currently exist or have existed in the past. As with the Krauthammer essay, you might ask students to consider how Steele's argument might have been presented in terms of an evaluation, a speculation about causes or effects, or a proposal to solve a problem.

Reading for Meaning

Because this essay is long and complex, students will find it especially necessary to annotate carefully as they read and reread. Students are, as always, asked to consider Steele's purpose and audience, and to relate their own observations and experiences directly to his position. They are also invited to examine Steele's analysis of the effects of affirmative action, as well as the contrasting terms (innocence vs. power, intentions vs. effects) in which he presents his position.

Extending Meaning through Conversation. Because the issue of affirmative action is likely to be one about which students feel strongly, you might move among pairs or groups, making sure that conversations are not moving too far away from the text itself. Once students have further explored their understanding of the meaning of the essay by discussing amongst themselves, you could have one member of each group report to the class on the results of this activity.

Reading like a Writer: Arguing Directly for a Position Using Cause-Effect Reasoning

Once again, students will note that the analysis of effects figures prominently in Steele's argument against affirmative action. Many students will find Steele's specific examples of African Americans affected by affirmative action policies especially effective in supporting his position.

Considering Ideas for Your Own Writing

Students are invited to take on the challenge of writing about affirmative action or other issues of current or ongoing national importance. Reminders following a list of possible topics reiterate that students are responsible both for justifying their own positions on an issue and for anticipating the objections of those who may oppose those positions.

Jill Kuhn, Sex Education in Our Schools

The issue addressed in this position paper should be familiar to your students. It deals with the perennial question of whether schools should offer sex education courses. As many of your students will discover when they write their own position papers, Kuhn found that she needed to do some library research to understand others' arguments better and to substantiate her own position.

Reading for Meaning

Students are asked to consider Kuhn's purpose and audience, mentioned in the headnote to the essay. This section also invites students to connect their own experiences and beliefs to Kuhn's argument, examining how their responses to Kuhn's essay are influenced by their own backgrounds.

Extending Meaning through Conversation. As students continue to explore and develop their understanding of Kuhn's argument by discussing it with one or two other students, they will undoubtedly be referring to their own experiences with sex education. This will be a useful starting point for their discussions of the essay, but you may need to remind them of the purpose of the activity, drawing them back to the text itself.

Evaluating the Logic of an Argument (A Further Strategy for Reading for Meaning). Once again, we refer students to Appendix 1: A Catalog of Critical Reading Strategies. Encourage students to devote their full attention to this activity, as it draws attention to crucial elements of the genre. This section of the appendix points out that the support for a writer's claim must be appropriate, believable, consistent, and complete; here, we ask students to evaluate Kuhn's argument to see whether it meets these criteria.

Reading like a Writer: Making an Essay Readable

Most students will note that Kuhn's argument is divided into three sections—three reasons that support her claim. Each reason (that parents are providing sex education ineffectively or not at all, that sexually active adolescents are often ignorant, and that AIDS makes sex education a necessity, especially for adolescents) is supported with references to authorities on the subject. Two references to then-Surgeon General C. Everett Koop—a prominent supporter of Kuhn's position—form an effective frame for her argument.

Compare. Once again, we ask students to focus on a particular feature of a genre by comparing different writers' use of similar strategies. You might help students get started with this activity by suggesting that they make a scratch outline of Kuhn's essay, identifying the features mentioned in the exercise, and that they then make a similar outline of a second essay from the chapter.

Reading like a Writer: A Follow-up Activity

By the time students complete this last section in the chapter of Reading like a Writer activities, they will have produced a rich amount of writing about this type of essay. Don't overlook the usefulness of having them select one of their responses to revise and extend through further analysis, thus reviewing and reinforcing what they have learned about the genre. They would then turn in this expanded piece as part of their final essay folders or end-of-course portfolios.

Considering Ideas for Your Own Writing

Students should be able to think of many issues relating to teenagers or young adults. They may also have had direct experience that relates to such issues. You might want to devote some class time to discussing these possibilities because students will be able to help each other and generate and consider topics.

THINKING ABOUT WHAT MAKES POSITION PAPERS EFFECTIVE

We ask students to focus on the central features of effective position papers, introduced following the sample essay at the beginning of the chapter, and to select the essay in the chapter that they feel best illustrates these features. You might have students who identify the same essay as most successful complete this activity as a group, perhaps sharing their responses in class as a way of facilitating a discussion of the genre.

A GUIDE TO WRITING POSITION PAPERS

The guide leads students through a composing process for position papers that follows these steps:

Invention
  Choosing an Arguable Issue
  Analyzing Your Readers
      Learning More about Your Readers: A Collaborative Activity
  Tentatively Stating Your Thesis
  Exploring Your Reasons
  Restating Your Thesis

Students should choose an issue on which they have already formed an opinion. If they are unsure of their position on an issue, students may substitute for their own thinking the position and arguments of someone who has already written on the issue, or their essays may merely summarize the two opposed points of view without siding with either. Students must establish and support a position, and that position should not be on the fence.

Other chapters have mentioned the importance of the invention step of analyzing readers, particularly because many readers are unaccustomed to the idea of writing to anyone besides their teachers. Even if they do grasp the need to address readers other than their instructors, their initial formulations of audience may be vague, general, and ill-defined. Since their position papers may be addressed to readers who hold an opposite position, and since the success of the paper depends on its ability to convince readers of the sense in the writer's position, understanding who these readers are and how they are likely to react is exceedingly important in a position paper.

The guide reminds students to think about their readers throughout the composing process, but you might give this initial step of analyzing readers some special attention, perhaps using student topics as examples to demonstrate the importance of accurately assessing an audience's knowledge, values, and positions on the issue. You might even play the role of a skeptical or opinionated audience to give students a sense of how their arguments might run into difficulties if they do not consider their readers carefully.

It is sometimes helpful to point to the painstaking market research routinely conducted in the business world as a practical example of "analyzing readers." Students should realize that considering an audience is an essential skill in the workplace and in all situations where they want to communicate their ideas to others. The invention process for the position paper stresses the need to identify the assumptions or values on which readers' opinions are based, and to look for assumptions and values the writer shares with readers as a means of opening communication between the opposed positions.

As they develop support for their best reasons, remind students to analyze their reasoning. Advise them to reread Evaluating the Logic of an Argument in Appendix 1: A Catalog of Critical Reading Strategies. Students should be aware of whether their appeals are mainly logical or emotional, and on what kind of evidence they are relying. Urge them to try to anticipate readers' objections and look for ways to refute or, possibly, accommodate them. From the essays in this chapter, they should have learned that the pattern of concession plus rebuttal is an essential one in argument.

When advising students on setting goals for their position papers, remind them that for some issues it is unrealistic to seek to change readers' minds. This is an important point, because students often believe that the objective of a position paper is to prove the opposition wrong. In fact, many position papers have much more modest goals, setting out merely to convince an entrenched opposition that the writer's position is reasonable and deserves more serious consideration and respect. Readers may finally disagree with the writer, but a position paper will have served a valuable purpose if they gain a better understanding of the writer's position and a more tolerant attitude toward it.

SPECIAL PROBLEMS OF THIS WRITING ASSIGNMENT. Probably the greatest problem students encounter when they begin writing position papers is mistaking assertion for argumentation. This problem manifests itself in sweeping generalizations unsupported by reasons and evidence. Students with little experience developing an argument usually assume that all they need do is state what they think. They don't realize that they have to give the reasons for their position and offer various kinds of evidence to support it. Nor do they recognize how important it is to anticipate readers' objections and questions and then either to modify their own position by acknowledging reasonable objections or to defend it by refuting unreasonable ones.

For some students, the essential problem is lack of experience in reasoning. Some students simply may be unused to setting out their reasons in a way that others can follow. For them, reading a diversity of arguments will provide instructive models. If, however, the problem stems from a lack of thoughtfulness, from the habit of relying on unexamined assumptions and biases, then the solution becomes more difficult. These students need first to accept the value of introspection and logical reasoning. They must recognize that the aim of argumentation is not merely to voice your own opinion but to examine it critically.

The root of the problem might be cognitive as well as emotional immaturity. Students who have not yet overcome their own egotism may have little experience with other points of view; therefore, they have few strategies for self-analysis, let alone for audience analysis. They may be able to assert their own opinions forcefully, but tend to have difficulty looking critically at their own assumptions or describing carefully their own train of thought. In our experience, students with this kind of problem respond well when argumentative writing is presented as an act of communication rather than as an act of aggression. When the emphasis is on creating common ground instead of squashing your opponents into the ground, students feel less defensive and more open to alternative ways of seeing.

PROMISING AND UNPROMISING TOPICS. We have found that there is no simple rule for prejudging the promise of topics for position papers. Many experienced instructors feel differently; for example, they often eliminate from consideration issues having to do with matters of faith like abortion and creationism. We find, however, that students can handle issues such as these reasonably if they take seriously other points of view. What we find most limiting is lack of information. If students are not well informed about a topic and do not have time or inclination to inform themselves, then their argument is likely to be fatuous—full of generalization and lacking in reasons and evidence.

Without making the assignment a full-blown research project, you might encourage students to discuss the issue with others and to do some reading about it. Exploring opposing views should be a natural part of the invention process. Sometimes, however, students make their research one-sided. It is good to seek reasons and evidence to support a position, but students also need to learn about the other side. They need to be able to anticipate objections and to appeal to values and concerns they share with others.

In the guide to writing, we offer a list of possibilities to get students thinking about issues they could write about. Many of the topics we suggest are ones we think students will know and also care about. Caring about the topic is essential for good writing, particularly for argumentative writing. This requirement comes as a surprise to some students and may even be threatening to them.

We have been amazed at the number of students who are reluctant to express an opinion. Many have been taught that it is inappropriate for them to do so. Some have been made to feel that they know too little to have an opinion worth sharing. Others believe that they are in college to consume ideas and opinions, not to produce them. For these students, we emphasize the process over the product. We explain that taking a position teaches them to analyze issues critically and to evaluate arguments pro and con. With experience, students gain confidence in their reasoning abilities and come to enjoy developing a thoughtful, well-supported argument.

Part 7 BIBLIOGRAPHIES

The following selected bibliographies, brief as they are, will remind experienced colleagues of the published resources in the field. They will also provide newcomers with a starting point for serious reading in composition studies and on learning from text.

COMPOSITION STUDIES JOURNALS. To follow new theory and pedagogy, writing instructors read these journals:

College English
College Composition and Communication
Journal of Advanced Composition
Rhetoric Review
Rhetoric Society Quarterly

Journal of Basic Writing
The Writing Instructor
Journal of Teaching Writing
Writing Program Administration
Journal of English Teaching Techniques
Teaching English in the Two-Year College

HISTORICAL SOURCES. Composition studies have a rich historical tradition reaching back to Greece in the fifth century B.C.E. The selections in this category highlight the major works from classical times, the English Renaissance, and the nineteenth century. All are currently available in reprints, most as paperbacks.

Plato, *Gorgias* (387 B.C.E.); *Phaedrus* (370 B.C.E.)
Aristotle, *Rhetoric* (335 B.C.E.)
Cicero, *De Inventione* (87 B.C.E.); *De Oratore* (55 B.C.E.)
Quintilian, *Institutio Oratoria* (95)
Erasmus, *On Copia of Words* (1512)
Wilson, *The Arte of Rhetorique* (1553)
Ramus, *The Logic* (1574)
Bacon, *The Advancement of Learning* (1605)
Campbell, *The Philosophy of Rhetoric* (1776)
Blair, *Lectures on Rhetoric and Belles Lettres* (1783)
Day, *Elements of the Art of Rhetoric* (1850)

RECENT HISTORICAL STUDIES. There has been a resurgence of interest in the history of writing instruction in American schools and colleges.

Berlin, J. A. (1984). *Writing instruction in nineteenth-century American colleges.* Carbondale: Southern Illinois University Press.
Berlin, J. A. (1987). *Rhetoric and reality: Writing instruction in American colleges, 1900–1985.* Carbondale: Southern Illinois University Press.
Connors, R. J., Ede, L. S., and Lunsford, A. A. (Eds.). (1984). *Essays on classical rhetoric and modern discourse.* Carbondale: Southern Illinois University Press.
Crowley, S. (1990). *The methodical memory: Invention in current-traditional rhetoric.* Carbondale: Southern Illinois University Press.
Horner, W. B. (1983). *The present state of scholarship in historical and contemporary rhetoric.* Columbia: University of Missouri Press.
Johnson, N. (1991). *Nineteenth-century rhetoric in North America.* Carbondale: Southern Illinois University Press.
Murphy, J. J. (Ed.). (1983). *Renaissance eloquence: Studies in the theory and practice of Renaissance rhetoric.* Berkeley: University of California Press.
Murphy, J. J. (Ed.). (1982). *The rhetorical tradition and modern writing.* New York: Modern Language Association.
Murphy, J. J. (1983). *A synoptic history of classical rhetoric.* Davis, CA: Hermagoras Press.

MODERN DISCOURSE THEORY. Modern theorists study the nature of written discourse, seeking to classify its many forms and to understand particular forms better.

Beale, W. H. (1987). *A pragmatic theory of rhetoric.* Carbondale: Southern Illinois University Press.

Britton, J., Burgess, T., Martin, N., McLeod, A., and Rosen, H. (1975). *The development of writing abilities (11–18).* London: Macmillan.

Burke, K. (1950, 1969). *A rhetoric of motives.* Berkeley: University of California Press.

Crusius, T. W. (1989). *Discourse: A critique and synthesis of major theories.* New York: Modern Language Association.

Kinneavy, J. L. (1971). *A theory of discourse.* New York: W. W. Norton.

Moffett, J. (1981). *Active voice.* Montclair: Boynton/Cook.

Perelman, C., and Ulbrechts-Tyteca, L. (First published in French in 1958. Translated and published in English in 1969.) *The new rhetoric: A treatise on argumentation.* Notre Dame: University of Notre Dame Press.

Toulmin, S. (1958). *The uses of argument.* Cambridge: Cambridge University Press.

RESEARCH. To follow research developments in composition studies, you would want to read two journals:

Research in the Teaching of English
Written Communication: A Quarterly Journal of Research Theory and Applications

Here we mention just a few recent book-length research reports, reviews of research, or collections of research studies:

Applebee, A. N. (Ed.). (1984). *Contexts for learning to write: Studies of secondary school instruction.* Norwood, NJ: Ablex.

Barton, D., and Ivanic, R. (Eds.). (1991). *Writing in the community.* Thousand Oaks, CA: Sage.

Beach, R., and Bridwell, L. S. (1984). *New directions in composition research.* New York: Guilford Press.

Beaugrande, R. de. (1984). *Text production: Toward a science of composition.* Norwood, NJ: Ablex.

Britton, B. K., and Black, J. B. (Eds.). (1985). *Understanding expository text.* Hillsdale, NJ: Lawrence Erlbaum.

Chafe, W. L. (Ed.). (1980). *The pear stories: Cognitive, cultural, and linguistic aspects of narrative production.* Norwood, NJ: Ablex.

Christensen, F. (1967). *Notes toward a new rhetoric.* New York: Harper & Row.

Cooper, C. R., and Greenbaum, S. (Eds.). (1986). *Studying writing: Linguistic approaches.* Newbury Park, CA: Sage.

Cooper, C. R., and Odell, L. (Eds.). (1978). *Research on composing: Points of departure.* Urbana, IL: National Council of Teachers of English.

Couture, B. (Ed.) (1986). *Functional approaches to writing.* Norwood, NJ: Ablex.

Dijk, T. A. van. (1980). *Macrostructure: An interdisciplinary study of global structures in discourse, interaction, and cognition.* Hillsdale, NJ: Lawrence Erlbaum.

Dillon, G. (1981). *Constructing texts*. Bloomington: Indiana University Press.

Freedman, S. W. (1985). *The acquisition of written language: Response and revision*. New York: Academic Press.

Halliday, M. A. K., and Hasan, R. (1976). *Cohesion in English*. New York: Longman.

Heath, S. B. (1983). *Ways with words*. New York: Cambridge University Press.

Hillocks, G., Jr. (1986). *Research on written composition*. Urbana, IL: National Council of Teachers of English.

Kirsch, G., and Sullivan, P. (1992). *Methods and methodology in composition studies*. Carbondale: Southern Illinois University Press.

Martlew, M. (Ed.). (1983). *The psychology of written language*. New York: John Wiley.

McClelland, B. W., and Donovan, T. R. (Eds.). (1985). *Perspectives on research and scholarship in composition*. New York: Modern Language Association.

McDonald, S. P. (1994). *Professional academic writing in the humanities and social sciences*. Carbondale: Southern Illinois University Press.

Nystrand, M. (Ed.). (1982). *What writers know: The language, process, and structure of written discourse*. New York: Academic Press.

Odell, L., and Goswami, D. (Eds.). (1985). *Writing in nonacademic settings*. New York: Guilford.

Purves, A. C. (Ed.). (1988). *Writing across languages and culture: Issues in contrastive rhetoric*. Newbury Park, CA: Sage.

Rose, M. (Ed.). (1985). *When a writer can't write: Studies in writer's block and composing-process problems*. New York: Guilford.

Scinto, L. F. M. (1986). *Written language and psychological development*. New York: Academic Press.

Smagorinsky, P. (Ed.). (1994). *Speaking about writing: Reflections on research methodology*. Thousand Oaks, CA: Sage.

Walvord, B. E., and McCarthy, L. (1990). *Thinking and writing in college: A naturalistic study in four disciplines*. Urbana, IL: National Council of Teachers of English.

Important research studies have appeared in two continuing-research monograph series:

Urbana, IL: National Council of Teachers of English for the Committee on Research:

Applebee, A. (1981). *Writing in the secondary school*.

Emig, J. (1971). *Composing processes of twelfth graders*.

Langer, J. A., and Applebee, A. N. (1987). *How writing shapes thinking*.

Mellon, J. C. (1969). *Transformational sentence-combining*.

Carbondale: Southern Illinois University Press for the Conference on College Composition and Communication:

Gere, A. R. (1987). *Writing groups: History, theory, and implications*.

Halpern, J. W., and Liffett, S. (1984). *Computers and composing*.

Kirsch, G. (1993). *Women writing the academy: Audience, authority, and transformation*.

LeFevre, K. B. (1987). *Invention as a social act.*

Markels, R. B. (1984). *A new rhetoric on cohesion in expository paragraphs.*

Rose, M. (1984). *Writer's block: The cognitive dimension.*

TEACHING PRACTICES. We have learned so much about teaching writing from so many different people that we would like to acknowledge them all here with references. But we must limit ourselves to just a few books that would be good starting points for beginning instructors. We are exceedingly rich in reported practice in composition studies:

Anson, C. M. (Ed.). (1989). *Writing and response.* Urbana, IL: National Council of Teachers of English.

Cope, B., and Kalantzis, M. (Eds.). (1993). *The powers of literacy: A genre approach to teaching writing.* Pittsburgh: University of Pittsburgh Press.

Elbow, P. (1981). *Writing with power.* New York: Oxford University Press.

Freedman, A., and Medway, P. (Ed.). *Learning and teaching genre.* Portsmouth, NH: Heinemann.

Graves, D. H. (1983). *Writing: Teachers and students at work.* Portsmouth, NH: Heinemann.

Hillocks, G., Jr. (1995). *Teaching writing as reflective practice.* New York: Teachers CollegePress.

Moffett, J. (1969, 1983). *Teaching the universe of discourse.* Boston: Houghton Mifflin.

Moran, C., and Herrington, A. (Eds.). (1992). *Writing, teaching, and learning in the disciplines.* New York: Modern Language Association.

Murray, D. M. (1985). *A writer teaches writing.* (2nd ed.). Boston: Houghton Mifflin.

Olson, G. A. (Ed.). (1984). *Writing centers: Theory and administration.* Urbana, IL: National Council of Teachers of English.

Secor, M., and Charney, D. (Eds.). (1992). *Constructing rhetorical education.* Carbondale: Southern Illinois University Press.

EVALUATION. These are good starting points:

Black, L., Daiker, D., Sommers, J., and Stygall, G. (Eds.). (1994). *New directions in portfolio assessment.* Portsmouth, NH: Heinemann.

Cooper, C. R., and Odell, L. (Eds.). (1977). *Evaluating writing.* Urbana, IL: National Council of Teachers of English.

Davis, B. G., Scriven, M., and Thomas, S. (1987). *The evaluation of composition instruction.* New York: Teachers College Press.

Gorman, T. P., Purves, A. C., and Degenhart, R. E. (Eds.). (1988). *The IEA study of written composition I: The international writing tasks and scoring scales.* New York: Pergamon Press.

Greenberg, K. L., Wiener, H. S., and Donovan, R. A. (Eds.). (1986). *Writing assessment: Issues and strategies.* New York: Longman.

White, Edward M. (1994). *Teaching and assessing writing.* (2nd ed.) San Francisco: Jossey-Bass.

Witte, S. P., and Faigley, L. (1983). *Evaluating college writing programs.* Carbondale: Southern Illinois University Press.

Applebee, A. N. (1984). Writing and reasoning. *Review of Educational Research*, 54, 577–596. This important review, while insisting on how little we know for certain about the role of writing in learning, argues that we may confidently infer from recent research and theory that writing fosters understanding and recall of reading, as well as the use of reading in new situations. Reviewed studies examine the influence on reading of writing answers to questions, notetaking, summarizing, paraphrasing, and analogizing.

Anderson, T. H., and Armbruster, B. B. (1984). Studying. In P. D. Pearson (Ed.), *Handbook on reading research* (pp. 657–679). New York: Longman. This comprehensive review examines the research support for several common studying techniques: underlining, notetaking, summarizing, questioning, outlining, and schematizing. The authors conclude that all of these techniques can enhance students' understanding and use of reading materials, but only if students are trained in their use and encouraged to use them purposefully. The most demanding uses for reading are best used through outlining and schematizing, the most time-consuming study techniques.

Baker, L., and Brown, A. L. (1984). Metacognitive skills and reading. In P. D. Pearson (Ed.), *Handbook on reading research* (pp. 353–394). New York: Longman. This review argues that self-monitoring during reading ("checking one's own cognitive activities") is essential for confident, productive reading. Comprehension monitoring, the research indicates, improves when readers can ask themselves questions (as in annotating a text), bring any relevant current knowledge to bear on the reading (as in previewing), recognize the main ideas (learned from summarizing texts), and follow the structure (learned from outlining texts).

Dole, J. A., Duffy, G. G., Roehler, L. R., and Pearson, P. D. (1991). Reading comprehension instruction. *Review of Educational Research*, 61, 239–264. After a wide-ranging theory review, effective reading comprehension instruction is conceptualized as depending on a set of five proven comprehension strategies: determining important information, summarizing information, drawing inferences, generating questions, and monitoring comprehension.

Glover, J. A., Plake, B. S., Robert, B., Aimmer, J. W., and Palmere, J. (1981). Distinctiveness of encoding: The effects of paraphrasing and drawing inferences on memory from prose. *Journal of Educational Psychology*, 73, 736–744. Two studies of college students support the conclusion that "what readers remember from reading passages is determined by the activities they engage in during reading." The researchers found that two activities were especially productive: paraphrasing and making inferences after paragraphs or brief sections.

Haller, E. P., Child, D. A., and Walberg, H. J. (1988). Can comprehension be taught? A quantitative synthesis of "metacognitive" studies. *Educational Researcher*, 17, 5–8. This review of twenty studies found that certain question-asking and writing activities (self-questioning, paraphrasing, summarizing, making predictions, integrating prior knowledge, awareness of text organization, comparing or contrasting main ideas) increase comprehension. Students in the studies were in elementary and secondary schools.

Kennedy, M. L. (1985). The composing process of college students writing from sources. *Written Communication*, 2, 434–456. This study of writing from sources analyzed the reading and writing strategies of six college students who were asked to write an essay about three articles on communication. The writing sessions were recorded in thinking-aloud protocols. Contrasting strategies of the three students with high-scoring essays to the three students with low-scoring essays, the researcher noticed that the successful writers were much more likely to paraphrase, summarize, evaluate, and annotate as they worked with the readings.

King, A. (1992). Comparison of self-questioning, summarizing, and notetaking-review as strategies of learning from lectures. *American Educational Research Journal*, 29, 303–323. Self-questioning and summarizing enabled underprepared college students to recall more from lectures and to remember it longer. Self-questioning was the most successful for long-term retention. Students were carefully trained to use these two productive strategies.

Langer, J. A., and Applebee, A. N. (1987). *How writing shapes thinking*. Urbana, IL: National Council of Teachers of English. In an ambitious, comprehensive study of writing in secondary schools, the authors learned that many kinds of writing activities (short-answer, summaries, notetaking, extended essays) enable students to learn more from their reading than if they had merely read or studied it. They also learned that different kinds of writing lead to different kinds of learning; summary, for example, to a comprehensive but superficial focus on reading material and extended essays to "deeper meaning about less information."

Marshall, J. D. (1987). The effects of writing on students' understanding of literary texts. *Research in the Teaching of English*, 21, 30–63. Eleventh-grade students wrote study-question answers, personal essays, and analytic essays about short stories. Students learned more about the stories when they wrote extended personal or analytic essays about the stories. In extended writing, students "construct an intellectual representation of the story—a representation that may stay with them and become for them, finally, the basis for what is remembered and understood about the story over time."

Newell, G. E. (1984). Learning from writing in two content areas: A case study/protocol analysis. *Research in the Teaching of English*, 18, 265–287. Eleventh-grade students read science and social science materials and then either took notes, answered study questions, or wrote extended essays. Students learned more concepts from the materials when they wrote essays. Essay writing "produced more writing and learning operations" and "required more extensive thought and consideration of content."

Simpson, M. L., and Nist, S. L. (1990). Textbook annotation: An effective and efficient study strategy for college students. *Journal of Reading*, 34, 122–129. One group of college students was given careful training in annotating, another group in previewing and then devising questions to guide reading. Both groups then were tested on knowledge of three 3,000 word passages they were given in advance to either annotate or devise questions about. Students who annotated performed better on the tests even though they reported spending less time studying.

Vacca, R. T. (1981). *Content area reading*. Boston: Little, Brown. Current texts on reading and study skills instruction provide useful catalogs of research-supported methods, many of them involving writing. Chapter 7 in this typical text presents strategies for previewing and analyzing reading through questions and discussions. Chapter 8 reviews several types of outlining and notetaking.

Wong, B. Y. L. (1985). Self-questioning instructional research: A review. *Review of Educational Research*, 55, 227–268. This theory-based review of twenty-seven studies (seventeen of them involving secondary-school or college students) concludes that when students ask themselves questions as they read, they process prose more confidently and comprehend it more fully. These studies examine the usefulness of three types of self-questions: to reflect on relevant prior knowledge, to understand the content, and to monitor understanding while reading.